A WATCH IN THE NIGHT

a WATCH *in the* NIGHT

THE STORY OF POMQUET ISLAND'S LAST LIGHTKEEPING FAMILY

RUTH EDGETT

NIMBUS
PUBLISHING

Nimbus Publishing Limited
PO Box 9166
Halifax, NS B3K 5M8
(902) 455-4286

Printed and bound in Canada

Cover and Interior Design: John van der Woude
Author photo: Eeva Miller

Library and Archives Canada Cataloguing in Publication

Edgett, Ruth, 1958-
A watch in the night : the story of Pomquet Island's last
lightkeeping family / Ruth Edgett.
Includes bibliographical references.
ISBN 13: 978-1-55109-611-7
ISBN 10: 1-55109-611-0

1. Millar, George. 2. Millar family. 3. Lighthouses—Nova Scotia—
Pomquet Island—History. 4. Pomquet Island (N.S.)—History. 5. Pomquet
Island (N.S.)—Biography. 6. Lighthouse tenders—Nova Scotia—Pomquet
Island—Biography. I. Title.

VK1140.M54E34 2007   971.6'14   C2007-900986-7

We acknowledge the financial support of the Government of Canada
through the Book Publishing Industry Development Program (BPIDP)
and the Canada Council, and of the Province of Nova Scotia through the
Department of Tourism, Culture and Heritage for our publishing activities.

IN MEMORY OF

George and Ruth Millar

*L*et us lay aside every weight,
and the sin which doth so easily beset us,
and let us run with patience
the race that is set before us.

— *Hebrews 12:1*

ACKNOWLEDGEMENTS

*P*eople are not born extraordinary. They prove themselves extraordinary in the way they respond to the world and the events around them. This book arises from the lives of eight extraordinary people: George and Ruth Millar and their children, Thelma, Rosa, Malcolm, Minna, David, and Barbara. It is based on their published and unpublished memoirs.

The stories that follow give glimpses of life in one Nova Scotia lightkeeping family. They are mostly reconstructions of actual events, although a good deal of liberty has been taken in their telling. The

Millar family characters are representations, not exact portrayals. Liberties have also been taken with other characters. Some are based on people who were associated with the Millars and others are purely fictional, although family names common to the area have been used wherever possible. In no case are characters meant to be portrayed as they actually were.

I take full responsibility for errors of fact. This is not intended as a definitive lightkeeping history, nor is it meant as a precise memoir of the Millar family. Rather, it is a partly factual, partly fictional story of one family's experience with the lightkeeping life in Nova Scotia during the early part of the twentieth century.

This book was very much a family project. It would not have been possible without the kind indulgence and patient commentary of all six Millar children: Thelma Beairsto (my mother, who deserves particular thanks for her contributions and encouragement), Rosa Mattinson, Malcolm Millar, Minna Halloran, David Millar, and Barbara Millar. Each has written a personal account of life on Pomquet Island, and these were the seeds from which this book blossomed.

For their support and critiques, I thank my husband Scott Edgett and my sister Susan MacDonald, whose eye and ear for authenticity were invaluable. For helping shape the manuscript into something publishable, I thank Shelley Hyndman and Patrick Murphy.

For their research expertise, I thank Virginia Clark, Karen MacKay, Margaret Carter, Carl Vincent, and Elizabeth Vincent. For access to historic files, I thank Richard Flemming, Fisheries and Oceans Canada, the Department of National Defence, and Library and Archives Canada.

For their expertise on various subjects, I thank Terry James (oxen), Bob Bancroft (birds), Chris Mills and Noel Palmer (lights), and Laurel Bernard and the Nature Conservancy of Canada (flora, fauna, and other details).

For one last visit to Pomquet Island with Thelma Beairsto on a beautiful summer day in 2005, Susan MacDonald, my mother, and I thank Andrew Williams of Helico Flight Services, Trenton, Nova Scotia.

Table of Contents

POMQUET ISLAND

Cranberry patch & spruce trees:
Faith, Hope & Charity ✷ ✷ *Seal Rocks*

✷ *well*

Track from Landing ——— ✷

✷ *Anchorage for*
George's lobster boat

The Landing ✷

Sand Bar

↖

Breakwater

◊

Bayfield Wharf
✷ .
. : *Irving's Lobster Cannery*

BAYFIELD BEACH

✷

BAYFIELD

✷ *Bayfield School House*
(now converted to a home)

NOVA SCOTIA

The first lighthouse—which is the present one with a few alterations during the years—was built in 1868. In those days it was much more of an undertaking, minus all the tools, machinery, and equipment of the present day.
—George Millar

A Safe and Commodious Harbour

PROLOGUE

Finally, the beast could touch bottom. He'd been swimming for a good half hour, panicking, not knowing where he was going or whether he would survive the next wave breaking over his up-stretched nose. His eyes were wild. As he gained ground and emerged streaming from the choppy sea, Jack the ox bellowed with all he had left in his lungs. Then he shook his great, horned head and trotted for shore.

An arc of water splashed into the rowboat that had just pulled alongside.

"Get out there and head him off! Quick!" The foreman was waving his arms where he sat in a small vessel that was not much longer than the beast himself. The craft had barely nosed the shoal before the young oarsman was over the bow, into the water, and gaining on the ox, holding his paddle high.

"Get back here you big bugger!"

Jack was heading for a spruce thicket that fringed the rocky beach. Ian Randall, soaked to the hips, leather boots gushing water with every step, put on a burst of speed and managed to get between the beast and the only thing that looked like a trail. It was a gap of sorts between the trees and a crop of scrubby shrubs hugging the edge of a low, red bank. The ox planted his front feet and rolled his eyes at Randall, sides heaving. Man and beast stood reckoning each other, heads lowered, water dripping. Neither had much left in him. It had been a long thirty minutes, with young Randall paddling hard in a crooked line to keep up with the ox while his boss used a long pole to prod the beast in the general direction of Pomquet Island.

"Aw, ta hell with it!" Randall knew oxen after all. He dropped the oar and reached for a short rope that still hung around the ox's horns. "C'mon ya dumb animal, we're not gonna kill ya." Randall gave the rope a tug and took a step in the direction they had just come. "Over here." Recognizing familiar instruction, the ox became suddenly docile and began to walk with his young captor. "You've got some haulin' ta do."

Much more slowly, the pair made their way to the beach where they could welcome a scow piled high with planks and boards that was just now reaching the stone-studded shoal.

"Okay boys!" Locky McEachen, the foreman, was already on dry land and shouting to the men not yet docked. "Let's git this lot unloaded and go back fer the next one. We want everything over here by dark so we can start buildin' ta-marra first light."

The boss was watching his four other hired men manoeuvre the scow through the rocky shallows. As soon as they were close enough, the men heaved into the foreman's arms the first pieces of equipment that would be required: a single yoke and head pad for Jack the ox. There would be just enough time for the beast to catch his breath and bearings before he would be hitched up to the first load of construction materials and commanded to haul them a half mile through the trees to the northeastern tip of the island.

"We got us a lighthouse ta build, boys!" McEachen tossed the tangle of leather and wood to Randall, then pitched in with the unloading.

So that was it. Ian Randall had just been designated ox-man. He could see that coming from the other shore, being from a farm himself where his own father preferred oxen to horses for doing the heavy work. Randall was a bit miffed at first, because the assignment meant he wasn't being allowed to work shoulder to shoulder with the older men and learn a new trade of his own. But it might not be so bad, he realized, barking up the business end of a jumped-up Jersey all day. This would at least partly exempt him from hauling and heaving the hundreds of planks and boards that would have to be unloaded from the scow, reloaded onto a skid behind the ox, and unloaded and restacked again a half-mile away. He might as well get on with it, then. Randall began to organize the simple harness while Jack, grateful for something familiar, ardently offered his head to the yoke.

Many loads were hauled and many miles were walked that day. Jack worked hard enough that the hauling took less time than expected. At a good 1,200 pounds in weight, this ox was here because he could handle his share of a burden, either in a pair or by himself, and because he was willing to take orders from any ox-man who knew what he was doing. Jack was one of Armand Fougere's favourites, and Fougere was loathe to let him go—especially swimming to Pomquet Island with a bunch of strangers. It wasn't the beast's ability he was worried about; it was the strangers'. Still, they say every man has his price, and so does every steer. Five dollars sealed the deal.

"You bring 'im home the way I see 'im before me right now," instructed Fougere. "Ee's a damn fine ox—ee's one 'a my best—an' I want 'im back 'ere in good trim!"

By suppertime Ian Randall and the ox were on good terms, the morning swim and chase all but forgotten. If he had it to do again, though, the young man would not have chosen an ox with the same name as the snarky old builder, Jack Chisholm. The senior man couldn't find the humour in hearing his name commanded over and over by a youngster whose father wasn't even in his good books. But the others got a kick out of the tension between elder and youngster, and it added some good, clean amusement to a long, hard day.

At day's end, Jack was released from his burdens and McEachen ordered construction to begin.

"We've got time to stake it out and start diggin' before dark." He was already handing out sharpened sticks and shovels. "Let's get to it."

By eight o'clock, there was a good-sized pile of dirt and the makings of a hole that would eventually become a cellar. Two canvas tents that might have been retired sails shone white in the lowering sun. The men had all stopped work to get some supper before the light faded completely. Tonight, it was warmed-over bannock and baked beans made only yesterday and packed in a tight-lidded crock by the foreman's wife herself.

"I've always had a taste for Claudette's beans," spoke up Jack Chisholm through a mouthful of bannock and black tea. "But I'm gonna need more than that fer all the heftin' I'm gonna be doin' here."

Snarky or not, Chisholm was senior and a friend of McEachen's, so the others let him speak for them. They nodded in agreement.

"Yep. We're gonna need good meat," came Stu MacDonald's voice from the other side of the circle.

"Don't worry, boys." The foreman was still shovelling in his own supper. "It's taken care of."

McEachen put down his fork. With the hand that wasn't holding his tin plate, he picked up a smooth stone that had been resting by his boot. He ran his thumb over its rounded edges. When he had sopped up the last of his beans, drained his tea, and had a leak over the bank, the boss singled out his errand boy while the other four amused themselves around the fire with their pipes and their tales.

Dusk was thickening now, and Jack the ox was enjoying the peace of a warm August evening. For the first time all day, he was chewing at his leisure on a patch of sweet summer clover when young Randall came along.

"You bin a good lad, Jack. No doubt about that." He drew an appreciative eye over the animal's robust flesh. Then he sidled along the steer's rump and ran a sure hand along a caramel flank. The ox had come to an uneasy trust in Randall over the course of his labours. Today, Randall was the one who had told Jack what to do, so he looked to the man for directions. It was Jack's shock at being introduced to his first job of the day that had set them at odds. The ox had never seen that much water before in his life, never mind having to swim in it.

They'd tried leading and coaxing and prodding and pulling, but it turned out the only way to get Jack into the water and keep him there was to fan the men out on both sides and whack him so hard with a stick and an oar from the rowboat that he saw no alternative but the water. If they succeeded in hooking a line onto him as originally planned, he would only drag the boat over hell's half acre, so they settled on poking and beating him from behind. It was anyone's guess how Jack would react when faced with the same swim in the opposite direction.

The young man lowered his voice as he approached Jack's long-horned head, hand still lightly on the ox's hide. Dried sweat along the beast's neck was sticky to Randall's touch, and there was a soft gleam from the worn brass knobs at the tips of Jack's horns. The ox-man stooped closer to Jack's broad face. He could just feel a breeze on his cheeks from the animal's drooping ears as they moved involuntarily to baffle early dusk bugs. Down at the other end, his tail was keeping the same rhythm.

"I wish we didn't have to do this, Jack, but there's nothin' else for it." Randall was almost touching the beast's forehead with his own as he spoke. Bent double now to address his charge, the young man could make out the brown depth of the animal's large almond eyes. The ox's lashes lowered in a long, lazy blink and he pressed his nose to the ground unconcerned. There was enough clover for both of them if Randall wanted some.

Jack didn't even see the knife.

"All right, boys! It'll be steak fer breakfast ta-marra!"

The foreman tossed his whet stone into the cooking fire, and a shower of sparks punctuated his announcement. He was the only one in the rest of the crew whose eyes had followed Randall and a just-sharpened knife into the gathering mist of a late summer evening. He was the only other in the group to see Jack the ox sink to his knees.

The year was 1867, and Jack had just dragged the lumber that was going to be hewn and pegged to fashion a light station for Pomquet Island in St. George's Bay, Nova Scotia. Now he was going to feed the construction crew.

No one among the workers thought to record his labours and those of his mates on paper. These men were not likely conscious they were a part of history that others, more than 135 years later, would be curious to look back upon. What they knew was that they were earning decent wages—for a time at least. Perhaps some had built lighthouses before, like the one at Cape George, for instance, about twenty-five miles north along the coast at the western lip of St. George's Bay. Perhaps one or two of these men were among those who had petitioned the Nova Scotia legislature to have this lighthouse established. After all, it didn't hurt to grease more than one wheel at a time.

It may be that someone in government kept files of the bids received for the Pomquet Island job, the specifications for the materials, and possibly even the design of the lighthouse, but those records have been lost. Construction occurred just as Nova Scotia was joining Canadian Confederation, and just as jurisdictions were changing hands. Even if files were transferred to Ottawa along with responsibility for Maritime lights, they were likely lost in the great fire of 1916 that destroyed the entire centre block of Parliament.

Those who built the lighthouse probably knew why there had to be a beacon on Pomquet Island. Resting along Nova Scotia's north coast in the nook formed by Cape Breton to the east and the mainland to the west, St. George's Bay was not always a friendly sea. On more than one occasion, ships had come to grief in bad weather off Cape George at the bay's northwestern lip, or at the Cape Jack Shoal near the head of the bay. It was a busy navigation route—ships passed through St. George's Bay on their way to and from the Strait of Canso, which linked Nova Scotia's north and south shores. This was the heyday of marine trade around the east coast of a burgeoning nation. Lumber, coal, fish, and agricultural goods were flowing freely among these soon-to-be provinces; the whole region was prospering. But safe navigation relied on good reference points on land, ones that could be seen in good weather and in bad. Thus, it was also a boom-time for lighthouse building, particularly along the coasts of Nova Scotia.

It was against this backdrop that a group of merchants, seafaring men, and others with interests in St. George's Bay petitioned for a remedy to the hazards, both financial and physical, that they faced. The harbour at Bayfield on the southern shore of the bay provided good shelter during storms. The trouble was, it was hard to find after dark because the shoreline was so low. If a captain wasn't careful, he'd keep going until he hit the Cape Jack Shoal and run aground, or if he were headed in the opposite direction during an easterly blow, he might try to clear the bay altogether and run into trouble off Cape George. But there was a small island at the entrance to Bayfield Harbour, probably named for the community of Pomquet just a few miles to the west. If a light were stationed on the island, it could guide mariners to safety in bad weather and serve as a marker in good.

There were 130 petitioners in all. They described themselves as "ship owners, master mariners and other inhabitants of the County of Antigonish." On March 16, 1867, they officially requested Nova Scotia's Legislative Assembly to establish a light to mark Bayfield Harbour. This is how they made their case:

"That a large amount of Shipping consisting of vessels engaged in the coal trade and fisheries vessels bound to and from ports in Canada, New Brunswick and the Northern Coast of this Province passes through the Bay of St. George.

That owing to the prevalence of Northerly and Easterly winds in the fall and spring months, the navigation of said Bay is attended with dangers at such times.

That ships encountering a Northerly or Easterly gale in said Bay in the night time often sustain injury, and are sometimes lost in endeavouring to weather Cape George at the North Western extremity or a dangerous reef, the Cape Jack Ledge, at the South Eastern extremity thereof.

That the Harbour of Bayfield on the western side of said Bay nearly midway between Cape George and Cape Jack and under the lee of Pomquet Island is safe and commodious and easy of access in daylight.

That owing to the lowness of the land about said Harbour the want of a Lighthouse and consequent difficulty of finding said Harbour after dark, vessels in distress in said Bay are prevented from taking refuge in Bayfield as they otherwise would.

That if said port was properly lighted it would be resorted by a large number of vessels to avoid the difficulty and danger of weathering Cape George or the Cape Jack Ledge during the night.

That the establishment of a Lighthouse on Pomquet Island at the entrance of said Harbour would be of great benefit to Mariners and would render the navigation of said Bay comparatively safe at all seasons."

By June of the same year, the Nova Scotia Board of Works was calling in Halifax's *Morning Chronicle* for tenders to erect a lighthouse on "Pomket Island, County of Antigonish." A light at Cape George had already been established in 1861.

Construction on the Pomquet Island light may have begun by late summer, 1867, although an entry in *Belcher's Farmers Almanac* stated the light was still under construction in 1868. What is known is that 1868 was the year the station was put into service and a lightkeeper hired. His name was John A. Atwater, and he would be paid roughly $345 a year until his death in early 1877. Colin A. Chisholm took over that spring and served for thirteen years. He was followed in 1890 by Michael Murphy, who retired in 1923. The fourth and last keeper of the Pomquet Island light was George Edwin Millar, at a starting salary of $75 a month. He took the job in the spring of 1924 and watched the light for the next thirty-five years. When he extinguished the oil lamp for the last time in November 1959, he and the flame he tended were replaced by the automated light that still marks the island today. This book is about George Millar, his family, and their life with the light on Pomquet Island.

To look ahead for thirty-six years seems a long
voyage with lots of reefs and shoals with many an
unexpected storm, but it is 'like a watch in the night'
when it is past. —George Millar

Ice Cakes Ahoy!

CHAPTER ONE

*R*uth Millar was going on faith. She had to. She could not swim, yet here she was on this fine April morning with a toddler and a babe in arms about to step, for the first time, into a rowboat. There would be nothing but this wooden shell and her husband's word between them and the bitter grip of St. George's Bay.

She was standing on Bayfield wharf, eyes fixed on her destination a half mile away—or what she could see of it anyway. There, beyond the blinding white of sun-splashed ice pans and mirror-blue water, rested a small island. From her vantage point, she could see scrubby trees clinging to what looked like steep and rocky banks. It would be a stretch to think of that place as home.

The Millars and their long-time friend, Tuttle King, were not the only human beings about at Bayfield wharf on this early spring day, but they were the only ones whose vessel was readying for launch. Ice was still too plentiful for safe navigation, so the fishermen bustling around them occupied themselves with the dry-land work of getting their gear ready for the start of the lobster season, the first of May. Even they were not ready to venture out on the water just yet. The gulls were out, though. With their primary food source—the lobster cannery—idle for the winter months, they moved in quickly, calling to each other on the breeze, alerting each other to the possibility of a meal. One gull wheeled on an updraft just over Ruth's head. She squinted upward. "No scraps today."

The fingers of Ruth's free hand caught a strand of wind-loosened hair, then worked deftly to restore it to the bun at the back of her neck. "Guess I will need that hat after all. It's warm enough in the sun, but the wind off the water is cold." She was speaking to no one in particular.

She didn't have much time for vanity, but Ruth's hair was her pride. When she was small it had been almost white, like that of her daughters. Now that she was twenty-six, darker strands shot through with gold hung just below Ruth's waist when she didn't have them pulled up into a neat ball. Each night, she would take out the pins and brush her hair into a glossy curtain before taking it over one shoulder and carefully working it into a long braid.

Ruth had moved off from her husband and his friend. They were busy loading a small rowboat that rested easily in the water next to the pier. Sometimes she could hear their voices echo through the fat, tree-trunk piles that held the wharf immovable and supported a wooden deck about four feet above the waterline.

"Hand me that-there cord, George, an' I'll lash this here sack under the seat so it don't move around—in case yus hit a rough patch."

A wind gust cut through Ruth's thin wool coat and she shivered. The disquiet—she would not call it fear—rising within her was not so much for herself as for her children. Rosa was beginning to fuss, not from the cold but from the involuntary tightening of her mother's grip. Ruth looked down at a pink face, the only flesh visible through layers of home-knit jumper and blankets.

"At least the baby is warm enough. We did need that extra blanket…" Ruth was still speaking to no one in particular, so she trailed off. Like her husband, she was typically a woman of few words.

Just then, her husband's unusually playful voice turned Ruth's head. "Now, Thelma," George Millar advised as he knelt on the wharf in front of his eldest daughter, "it's your job to watch out for ice cakes. If you see any close to the boat, call out, 'Ice cakes ahoy!'"

His big hands were on her shoulders and her round, blue eyes seemed fastened to his as she nodded assent.

George hadn't taken his own gaze from Thelma's face, but Ruth knew by his tone that the next words were for her. "We can get in now." So she moved to join her husband at the lee side of the wharf.

"In you go!" George hoisted Thelma—not quite two-and-a-half years old—high into the air, then carefully lowered her into the bow of the four-person rowboat tied to the wharf. Thelma was standing inside the boat and George hadn't yet let go of her hands. He guided his daughter backwards until she was perched on a short wooden seat at the bow, her face to the stern.

"You sit there and put one hand on each side of the boat." Gently, he let go of the two small hands and Thelma did as she was told. "Just like that."

Maintaining the same even, gentle tone, her father instructed, "Sit right there and don't get up. Just stay there while Mum and Rosa get in too."

Wordlessly, Ruth handed Rosa to her husband, then did as he had drilled her earlier. Climb down the ladder from the wharf to the boat. Be careful to make as little movement as possible. Stay low and hold onto the sides. Step high over the middle two seats. Be careful not to trip on your coattails. Turn around very carefully and face the front, all the time holding onto the sides.

Ruth felt cold wood underneath as she lowered herself onto her seat at the stern. Now she was facing wide-eyed Thelma, whose tiny, mittened hands were gripping the gunwales a few feet away, just as her father had told her. Ruth smiled encouragement to her daughter, then looked up to George on the wharf and nodded as she held out her arms. George knelt, stretched downward as far as he could to close the gap between wharf and boat, and passed the baby to his wife. Simultaneously, Ruth stretched upward to the limit her height would allow without moving from her seat. She took the still-sleeping Rosa close and nodded another smile to Thelma.

"There now, Mrs. Millar, yer all set to go! You'll be on dry land before ya know it!"

Ruth nodded up toward Tuttle. She appreciated his effort to cheer her on, but she could see past his words quite clearly to the broken ice floes bobbing in the channel behind him. She fancied they looked like bits of cork as she watched them ride and bob on a gentle swell that rippled through the harbour. With Rosa balanced on her knees, she pulled a wool tam from her coat pocket and fit it over her head, quickly tucking her ears underneath. Her eyes went from Tuttle to George, whose turn was next.

Ruth was a petite match to her husband's bulk. His beguilement at her five-foot-three, 115-pound-frame was somewhat of a private joke between them. To others, he referred to her as "The Little Woman." In conversation—particularly when there was a possibility for disagreement, or when he was proposing something new—George often prefaced his remarks with, "Now, Little Woman…" In the presence of others, she called him George, but in her diaries and to herself, he was "Friend Hubby."

If husband and wife hadn't been so intent on their task this morning, George might have made some kind of remark about how Ruth and her two small children made hardly a whit of difference to the rowboat's bearing where it rested in the water. George and Tuttle had packed the space under the centre seats with three gunny sacks containing bedding, a few personal articles, and food rations for a week. But the combined weight of cargo, mother, and children still left the vessel sitting comparatively high in the water.

Now George climbed in. This time the added weight made a difference. At five foot ten and 185 pounds, George Millar was not a large man, but he was solid. The boat sunk closer to its waterline, wobbled a bit, and righted itself as he carefully lowered himself into the oarsman's seat. On George's signal, Tuttle untied the two lines securing the boat to the wharf and tossed them into the craft. George picked up one oar and pushed off from the wharf. Once the boat was safely gliding on the water, he took up the second and began pulling his family into their new life, one stroke at a time. It was 1924 and George Edwin Millar was about to become keeper of the Pomquet Island light. He would be taking up his new duties just as the navigation season reopened along the northern shores of Nova Scotia.

Tuttle watched them go, lifting an arm in their direction. "An' don't you worry about Jumbo, George. I'll keep 'im well 'til yer ready ta swim 'im over later on."

As he called out this parting message, Tuttle jerked his head backwards to indicate the big grey horse that stood patiently between the shafts of a small wagon a few yards off. Tuttle remained there at the tip of the wharf, arm half-raised, until he saw the boat rounding the breakwater about a quarter mile down the shore. He turned to Jumbo. "All right, boy, let's go home." Only then did Tuttle realize all work at the wharf had stopped. The eyes of some dozen fishermen were either turned to him or were following the small boat that was steadily shrinking into the distance with each pull George made on the oars.

What had Ruth been thinking when she agreed to this? The water was littered with ice farther than her eyes could see: first, St. George's Bay; beyond that the Northumberland Strait; and, beyond that, the North Atlantic Ocean. The bright sunlight was blinding at times, glinting off the sea and bouncing off brilliant white chunks of ice and snow. When they occasionally passed closely to a floating remnant of winter, she could see the ice was marbled with grit and layered by successive snowfalls and freezes.

With Rosa quiet inside her warm blankets and Thelma transfixed by the bow parting water before her, Ruth took a moment to shift in her hard seat and straighten her coat so that it better covered her stockinged legs. Now well away from the wharf, her practical Protestant mind told her that if she ever had meant to express doubts about this adventure, it was too late now.

It is possible that George—square jaw set, eyes on the picture of mainland slowly receding behind Ruth and the baby—could have been thinking along the same lines. She would never know. He would not tell her if he was.

George Millar's solid physique and dark colouring made him an imposing figure. He had full, dark hair and eyebrows, deep-set brown eyes, and a thick brush of a moustache that overhung a square chin. These physical features accented a no-nonsense aspect that probably came from having made his own way in life since the age of twelve, or from stumbling into manhood on the muddy battlefields of France. Whatever caused it, there was a definite air about George Millar that told others he did not suffer fools. Ruth knew his lighter side, but neither of them was in a joking mood today.

The Millars' new life was getting closer now: a kite-shaped outcropping of rock and scrub about a half-mile long and an eighth of a mile across at its widest. The island's edges were defined by cliffs of deep red in some parts and by large rocks in others. There was no beach, only grey and red rubble reaching into the shallows. For the life of her, Ruth could not see where they were going to land, but Michael Murphy before them had done it, so there must be a place. Besides, George seemed to know where he was going, and it was best not to distract him with questions. Ruth knew by the set of his jaw when he was concentrating on a problem, and he was concentrating now—on keeping as far as possible from the free floating pans of ice that surrounded them.

Perhaps if they had waited a day or two, a change in wind direction might have moved the ice completely out of the harbour. But a different wind might have pushed more ice in. Early on in their lightkeeping career, the Millars learned to take advantage of the weather when it was in their favour, however briefly that might be.

Ruth judged they had been at sea about twenty minutes when details of the Pomquet Island landing became clear. It was a low point at the tip of the island closest to the mainland breakwater, which stretched a quarter mile to the northwest of Bayfield wharf. Ruth could just begin to discern a rough road through the trees—if you could call them trees. The ones near the water's edge were more like a ragged hedge of small bushes and scrawny saplings, but she was relieved to see land coming closer with every stroke of the oars. Her feet were beginning to ice up, and the frigid air close to water level had risen under her dress. Even though pants would have been perfectly permissible under the circumstances, Ruth remained steadfastly skirted. In fact, she didn't own a single pair of pants.

Thelma wasn't minding the cold, though. She was still fascinated by new sights and sounds all around. She was tilting her head back to watch the half-dozen gulls that had been following the boat in lazy circles. The seabirds began screaming in earnest as they jockeyed for the possibility of food at the landing. The noise caused a flock of starlings to break cover in the trees and flee, chattering among themselves, to a less-threatening spot.

George let the boat nose as far as possible into the shallows before stepping out. Wading through water just below the tops of his gum rubber boots, he dragged the craft onto a narrow stretch of rock-cleared beach, then held out his hands to help Thelma from her eager perch. He deposited her on a dry patch and raised a hand in front of her. "You stay right here and don't move."

Now his tone held in it more of the authority that his children would come to recognize so well.

George waded back out to the boat and took Rosa so that Ruth could disembark. As she welcomed solid ground underfoot and baby back into her arms, Ruth turned around in time to catch Thelma by the collar. The child had been about to go into the water with her father, who was wrestling the boat farther up onto the landing in order to unload the family's provisions. He would bring some with him now as they walked the tree-shaded road to the lighthouse for the first time. With Ruth, Thelma, and Rosa safely delivered, George would come back for the rest.

As they approached the edge of the woods that marked the end of their second half-mile journey, Ruth set eyes for the first time on her family's final destination. At the outer-most tip of the island atop a fifty-foot cliff, having not a tree nor a shrub for shelter, stood a stark, white box of a house with a twenty-foot light tower fixed to one side.

Not that Ruth was accustomed to luxury. The youngest of a strict Presbyterian family in which only two of five children survived through adulthood, Ruth Elizabeth Mitchell had been raised austerely and had learned early in life to take adversity in stride. Losing her twelve-year-old sister Martha to an emergency appendectomy on the kitchen table while she herself was still a child may have gone some way to forging the invisible steel rod that kept her backbone straight and her eyes forward.

This daughter of first cousins David Mitchell and Minnie Wood still retained a life-long good humour, though. All who knew Ruth would say that she accepted both hardship and good fortune with equanimity. She had been unable to fulfill a childhood dream to become a teacher because her father did not believe in "educatin' women." His ambition for her was that she be a stay-at-home spinster in order to see her parents through old age. Her betrothal and marriage to George Millar were, then, the first clear evidence of a strong will at the core of an outwardly complaisant woman. In the end, her parents did not object to the wedding. Even if his upbringing was questionable, George seemed an honest lad—and he had fought for King and country after all.

These young partners had been acquainted since their school days in Pugwash, about 125 miles west of Bayfield, as the crow flies, along the Nova Scotia coast. Even after a teenaged George followed his widowed father to Manitoba on the harvest excursion train looking for work, and even while he was overseas during The Great War, George and Ruth kept up a correspondence.

No one who knew them would accuse either of being outwardly sentimental, but Ruth must have spent at least some time as a young woman gazing at that sepia print of a soldier in uniform. It was taken when George was eighteen, just before he shipped off for England with the 78 Battalion Winnipeg Grenadiers in November 1915. On the back of the photo were these words: "From one who cannot and will not forget you—George Millar." Their letter exchanges may not have been known to Ruth's parents, since Ruth was among many young Canadian women who wrote friendly letters to the boys overseas. But the romance that lay dormant during the war years blossomed quickly once the fighting was over.

Freshly—and by God's own hand, safely—delivered from battle, George had meant to buy a farm in Manitoba using the service bonus he had received upon discharge from the Canadian Expeditionary Force. He was about to buy two parcels of land when he returned to Pugwash for Ruth. Then came the second obvious act of will on Ruth's part: she would not leave her family in Nova Scotia, and she would not leave the sea. In one of the few compromises of his life, George made his choice. The young couple took up farming, supplemented by lobster fishing, at Pomquet Ferry next door to Bayfield, Nova Scotia. They were lured there by George's long-time friend Tuttle King, who was always in need of fishermen to supply his small lobster cannery.

But farming and fishing were not as lucrative as George had hoped. So, when Pomquet Island lightkeeper Michael Murphy retired and a friend recommended the job to young George, he took it. As a war veteran and a man of presumably dependable character, he was a preferred applicant. At seventy-five dollars a month, the salary would not make him rich, but it would provide a stable income and shelter for his growing family. Besides, he would still be able to fish lobster to supplement his wages, although he would now be supplying H. Fred Irving's cannery at Bayfield wharf.

As George, Ruth, and their children now neared their new home on Pomquet Island, they began to take inventory of the small cluster of buildings coming into view. The first and largest was the barn. It was located well away, and slightly uphill, from the lighthouse. Still farther uphill was the well, covered only by a wooden platform, from which drinking water was drawn by hand. Next were the pigpen, chicken coop and wood house, all joined together by fencing and chicken wire, and located a short walk from the back door of the lighthouse. On the opposite side of the residence, near the bank, was the oil house. This was where kerosene for the lighthouse lamp was stored in large metal drums. Completing the array of structures was an outhouse, just a few yards from the back door. All of these buildings—including the home—had been unoccupied since the close of the navigation season the previous January.

The closer they got to the house, the more Ruth could see the possibilities. Yes, it was exposed to the elements. There would be no fixing that, since the lighthouse and the beam from its lamp needed to be visible at sea from all angles. But, Ruth hoped, the chill on all but the windiest and coldest of days would be warmed away by the two stoves George had told her about: a wood-fired kitchen range and a pot-bellied stove in the parlour that could burn either coal or wood.

There was an air of standoffishness in the house's boxy straightness, but it was straight and that was good. There was a sturdy roof and a coat of whitewash that looked as though it had been renewed only last year. Given the yard's barren look, the keeper before them hadn't been much of a gardener, but there was lots of space for flower beds, and Ruth would make up for the previous proprietor's oversight as time and weather allowed.

Some way into their walk from the landing, George had hoisted a tiring Thelma onto one hip and wrestled the burden of supplies under his opposite arm. As they rounded the corner of the house to approach the front entrance, Ruth saw him kneel to lower Thelma, then the bundle, gently to the ground. No sooner did the canvas bag touch soil than George had to stretch to catch his daughter—again by the back of her coat—before she toddled toward the house. As he took her small hand in his and started explaining that this was her new home, Ruth noted the house was almost surrounded by cliffs and sea below. She saw how the ground just over her right shoulder fell away, showing nothing but rocky beach and water. She could hear small waves washing the shore below. George picked up the duffle bag and shepherded his family toward the entrance. Upon opening the front door, they discovered a horde of flies enjoying the warmth and sunlight of the south-facing vestibule.

Spring cleaning, then, would be Ruth's first order of business. George's would be tending to the light. The next thing would be settling in the livestock, including the work horse Tuttle King was keeping until the water warmed up. The only way to transport large animals like cattle and horses was to swim them to the island or walk them on the ice. The smaller ones—pigs and chickens—could travel by boat or scow, but only under smooth sailing conditions. George already had most of the animals he would need back on the farm at Pomquet Ferry, itself almost within hailing distance of the Pomquet Island landing. Neighbours would make sure they were cared for until he could move them to the island.

On opening the front door, we were met by a welcoming chorus: the buzzing of countless thousands of flies enjoying the warm sunlight. Had they known what was in store for them, I doubt if they would have sung so merrily!
—George Millar

Once inside the house it dawned on George, about the same time it did on Ruth, that her hands would be more than full keeping Thelma out of mischief while seeing to such immediate duties as watching a sleeping Rosa, shooing flies, and setting onto everything that couldn't fit into a washtub with elbow grease and a stiff-bristled brush.

"Thelma can come back to the landing with me." Then, to Ruth, "You can put Rosa over there."

George pointed to a sun-bathed patch of floor down the hall and to the left. Ruth moved toward it and nodded as though her husband had put voice to her own thoughts. She lowered Rosa onto the floor, then knelt to bank her on both sides with the bedding they had just brought from the landing. The baby's woolen cap and outside blanket could be loosened a bit now, since the sunlight was warm and they were sheltered indoors. Still, the winter chill in the house's bones kept Ruth from removing Rosa's outer clothes—or her own.

George and Thelma were out the door almost as soon as they had come in.

"Thelma, I need you to help me bring the rest of the things from the boat. Come with me."

Ruth heard the front door open and shut, then a frazzle of just-awakened spring flies as they struggled to retain their warm perches on the windowpanes of the front porch. Now she was free to explore, so she back-tracked to the front room.

Centred along one inside wall of the parlour was the pot-bellied stove she'd been told about. It came nearly to her shoulders and sat on a tin-covered platform about an inch thick. It was made of black cast iron and fashioned in the customary hour-glass shape. The plump sides of the top section were checkered with small windows that held opaque mica panes. These were strong enough to withstand heat, yet translucent enough to give a warm, red glow when a fire was burning inside.

Ruth cocked the shiny nickel door handle and pulled it toward her. This was a mistake. Bits of spent coal and ash tumbled onto the painted boards of the floor. She slammed the door shut and latched it as quickly as she'd opened it. The stove would have to be cleaned before being lit again. But that would not likely be until the fall, so she would turn her attention to more urgent duties. Before moving on, though, Ruth paused to brush a hand over the nickel globe that topped the stove, like a dollop of icing on a chocolate cupcake. This room would be a place of warmth for her family.

Just across the entry hall from the parlour door was a stairway to the second floor, but Ruth would scout the downstairs first. She moved again to the room where Rosa lay, which she surmised must be for dining. From here, Ruth could see the kitchen at the rear of the house. She knew this because she could see a few cupboards, a white porcelain sink, and one corner of a kitchen range. She glanced at Rosa to assure herself the baby was still sleeping, then ventured to investigate further.

The range was a good stove, cast iron with nickel trim—just like the parlour stove—and much nicer than the one she'd left behind at Pomquet Ferry. She lifted one of the smooth, round lids that covered the firebox and peered in at the remainder of a charred stick of wood. There was a small, square door on the front for loading large sticks, and for cleaning away the remains. Over at the far right of the stovetop, Ruth noticed a rectangular lid that covered a tank to heat water for washing. About two and a half feet above all of this, supported on a sheet of cast iron that formed the back of the stove, was a warming oven. It stretched the length of the stove—roughly five feet—and overhung about one-third of its width. This would be the place for wet winter mittens, rising bread dough, and occasionally, meals awaiting George's arrival when unforeseen events made him late. But the handiest thing about this range, to Ruth's mind, was the two fold-down warming trays trimmed in nickel, just above the stovetop. She knew she would find good use for these. The oven door highlighted this softly sheened package of black and silver. Taking up about two-thirds of the stove front, the un-windowed door, too, was trimmed in nickel. At its centre, just below the handle, it bore the words, "Renfrew Vanity."

Ruth could judge that, by the temperature in the room and the lay of the floor a few inches lower than the rest of the house, this would be a summer kitchen only. It would likely be too cold for habitation in winter. In fact, she could see a stovepipe hole through the ceiling of the dining room and marks on the floor underneath that seemed to show where the range would have to be moved for the winter months. The previous light-keeper probably hadn't bothered to move it this last time, since the worst of winter would only have begun when it was time for him to leave.

Conspicuous by its absence in this kitchen was anything resembling a system for drawing water. Ruth recalled the non-mechanized, unsheltered well and large rain barrels she had seen positioned at the four corners of the house. This would not be an easy day—even for the daughter of a Presbyterian.

In a corner of the house made by the joining of the dining room and parlour was another empty room—a good place for overnight guests, perhaps. Opposite this door, and under the dining room window, Ruth could see a large rectangular hatch cut in the floor. She moved to inspect it and pulled the ring that served as a handle. She raised the cellar hatch only partially and smelled the damp mustiness of earth mingled with the faint odour of decayed vegetables—this was where the food would be put down for winter. Maybe tomorrow she would have a look down there. Descending into that darkness was not something she was prepared to do right now. The living space was enough to deal with on this first day, so she let the hatch drop back down with a soft thud.

The baby was still sleeping in the warm sun. One of two flies sampling her warm blanket flew off as her mother moved closer to make sure the noise hadn't disturbed her, but Rosa was oblivious to the soft buzzing. Seeing all was quiet, Ruth advanced to the stairway and emerged into a large hall brightened by a skylight. Up here were three doors leading to the bedrooms. The first two had dormer windows and the third, another skylight.

There was a fourth door that opened on a small room containing another stairwell that led to a trap door above Ruth's head. She wouldn't bother to negotiate these steps right now. She knew the third-storey room would be the lantern, the chamber in which the lighthouse lamp was housed. George could explore that later. Caring for that place would be his responsibility.

Ruth needed to get to her own job now, which was seeing that this cold, dusty house was fit for a young family to live in by bedtime. She closed the staircase door and made for the kitchen, where she would light a fire in the stove and dig out the cleaning supplies that had come in the first kit bag. She was ready to get to work, and she had decided one thing: the flies would be the first to go.

*At first, life on our island included only the bare
necessities of life, but gradually we became acclimatized,
and by trial-and-error method developed quite a
satisfactory way of life. This 'way of life' became part of
the warp and woof of our existence.* —George Millar

A Fixed Red Light

CHAPTER TWO

George and Thelma would deliver the remainder of provisions to the lighthouse on the next trip from the landing. By the time they reached the place where the remaining two gunny sacks had been left alongside the boat, Thelma was tired. George was going to have to carry her and sling the straps of the two large bags over his shoulders in order to get everything back to the house in one trip. Before hoisting his load, he knelt by one of the sacks and felt inside for the tin teapot he knew was near the top. Still kneeling, he turned to Thelma and, taking her small, mittened hands in his, appointed her keeper of the precious vessel.

"Here, you take this and be sure not to drop it."

Thelma nodded soberly and allowed George to mould her hands, one around the handle and one around the spout. At not even two-and-a-half, she understood the importance to her father of this drab and dimpled piece of kitchenware. She had seen him pick it up from the stove often enough, and she knew quite well the smell of strong and steaming tea that issued from it.

This trip would be slower than the first, with Thelma riding on her father's shoulders clasping the teapot while he pressed forward with the two bags hanging by their canvas straps. As they left the landing for their return trip, father and daughter cast a bouncy shadow on the ground, and Thelma could feel warm sun on her back. But just then a breeze lifted off the bay. It made George wish he had thought to turn down the ear lugs on his cap before he'd taken on his second load.

The track was narrow, rough, and mostly devoid of grass from generations of passage by man, beast, and contraption. George could make out the odd hoofprint in the partly frozen ground—here of a horse, there of a cow—left by previous occupants of this lonely place. Close-set spruce trees lined the way. At the edges of the island, the trees faced the sea wearing their green branches to the rear, protected from the scourging salt mist. To the water, they presented only mottled, grey bark and a few withered twigs. At the sides of the trail, sheltered from the sea air, their prickly needled branches kept all but the most determined at arms-length, away from the dark wood beyond. Today, the trees provided George and Thelma some protection from the wind, and by the time the pair reached the house, George was sweating.

Ruth was surprised by her relief at the return of her husband and daughter. She had been too busy getting acquainted with her new situation to be conscious of the loneliness in it. This feeling was not something to be dwelt upon, so she had made herself busy arranging Thelma for an overdue nap beside Rosa on the dining room floor. Now she was ready to confer with George about the things she'd discovered in his absence. Where was he, anyway?

By the time Ruth's search reached the back door, George was coming through it with a full bucket of icy water, which he sat directly on the stove top. It had taken some searching, but he had found the water bucket in the summer kitchen. He recognized it by the attached rope that would be used to lower it into the well. Now, he draped the rope over the warming oven to keep it out of danger. Ruth had already started a fire in the range using last year's leftover wood that had been stacked just inside the back door. There was now drinkable water, and the teapot had already been unpacked, so George fished around in a bag and pulled out a box of King Cole tea. It was time for the parents to take a rest.

An hour later, George could hear the bumping and clanking of Ruth's housekeeping through a stovepipe hole in the floor of the upstairs hall as he approached the object of his family's exercise: the light. It didn't take long to find the door that Ruth had discovered only a short time earlier. George entered the small room and mounted the steeply hung steps, careful to keep hold of the iron rails. To distract his mind from the steepness of his ascent, he kept his eyes on the metal trap door overhead. Soon, he could reach it with one free hand. He pushed it up and open and emerged into a square and all-but-empty room.

The kerosene smell hit him first. The air was thick with it. The room had not been disturbed since the lighthouse had been closed up for the winter four months previously. An ex-soldier's reconnoitre of the oilclothed floor told George no fuel had been spilled. It was simply the aroma of time in a room where a kerosene flame had been lit and extinguished every day of the navigation season for the past fifty-six years. The vent at the peak of the ceiling was efficient at drawing away smoke from the flame, but it did nothing to help air out the room without a cross-draft from an opened hatch.

George's first act was to pull back the heavy canvas curtains that covered three sides of the room. Sunlight now streamed through plate glass windows, which had already been warming this high space, even through the fabric. He glanced down to the oil shed in the yard below, ten or twenty paces from the house on the seaward side. He had already taken a brief look there while getting the water for Ruth. It smelled of kerosene, too, but in a more dangerous way: decades of leakage had soaked the shed's floor in oil. He would try to do something about that later. For now, he was glad the habit of smoking, which had comforted his trench buddies in France, hadn't stuck with him.

George took some time to stand, then, and absorb the atmosphere of this lofty observatory. It seemed a long way from the sea and the island below. On the ground, some evergreens close to the water waved in unison but George could hear no wind. Nor could he hear the white-capped waves releasing onto the rocks at the base of the cliff. He took a step backwards from the window and looked up. The sky was cloudless and sunlight bounced off the white window sashes. He could see gulls high in the distance but only faintly hear their screech-ing. The sun was warm on his face and he was starting to get used to the smell. There was a kind of peace to this high sanctuary under glass.

There were three gnarled and twisted spruce not far from the north bank which were named Faith, Hope, and Charity. Before we left, both Faith and Hope had died, but Charity still remained, which is ample proof that "the greatest of these is Charity."
—George Millar

Nearly as quickly as it came upon him, George shook off this broody moment and turned his attention to the centre of the fourteen-foot square room. There on an iron platform sat a large semi-circular piece of glass about a foot and a half in diameter and fixed in a polished brass frame. This was the lens that magnified the Pomquet Island light. George had to turn his head to avoid the slic-ing light of sun on glass as he moved to the rear opening. From here he could see a simple apparatus called a duplex burner. It consisted of a copper lamp that held one gallon of kerosene and two flat, cotton wicks. A colourless glass shade fit over the wicks, and over that shade fit another red one. At night, as the lamp burned inside the embrace of the lens, it sent out a steady red glow that was visible for nine miles at sea. This was how sailors knew Pomquet Island. It could be found at latitude 45° 39"40'N, longitude 61°44" 30'W. Mariners knew it as a "fixed red light."

This was the light around which George and Ruth Millar would fashion the next thirty-five years of their lives and those of their children. But for all that, the light was striking in neither aspect nor size. Pomquet Island's was a fifth-order light. It did not signal major landfall to vessels crossing the ocean, as a first- or second-order light would do, nor was it positioned in a major shipping lane. By 1924, the nineteenth-century tide of marine commerce that originally justified this lighthouse had ebbed considerably. Its main purpose now was to serve the fishermen of St. George's Bay.

The lightkeeper's mission was a simple one: to ensure the lamp burned through the night, so that every mariner who needed it could see it. To this end, George would light and extinguish the lamp at dusk and dawn; he would replenish the kerosene; he would trim the wick to prevent it from smoking; he would clean the shades and polish the lens to make the light shine brightly; he would clean the windows of the lantern house and keep the brass and copper work polished; and, he would keep a logbook in which he recorded the time and weather conditions with every lighting and every extinguishing of the flame. This George would do without fail every day of the navigation season between mid-April and mid-January, and he would accomplish it with military efficiency.

The young keeper could not resist an impulse to put his hand behind the glass and see how big it looked in a magnifier like this. The lens was the most intriguing part of the lighting apparatus. It was of a type invented by Frenchman Augustin Fresnel in the late 1700s. The Pomquet Island lens was a much smaller adaptation of the gigantic and intricate works of art that bore the Fresnel name at such major lights as Sambro Island, at the entrance to Halifax Harbour, and Cape Race, on the eastern coast of Newfoundland. Still, as Ruth would say, this smaller lens had its own peculiar beauty.

This lens operated on the same principles as its larger cousins. It focussed the lamp's flame by redirecting and magnifying the light. Normally, rays of light from a flame would shoot in all directions and be lost in the night sky a few hundred yards beyond the tower, but the Fresnel lens was able to capture these rays in concentric bevels around the top and bottom of its thick glass semicircle. These ridges directed the light horizontally while a large bullseye sandwiched between them magnified the kerosene light. The result was one strong beam sent seaward.

As he examined the giant glass eye, George saw how, by day, it directed the sun's rays in a reverse path toward the centre of the lamp. He quickly realized why the lantern house was curtained during daylight hours. In one stride, he reached a window facing directly into the sun and pulled the drape, which gave some relief to his eyes. As he pulled the drape, he noticed the iron-railed catwalk that ran around the outside of the room. Its access was a door directly behind the lamp, but he chose not to step out just yet. Instead he turned back to the centre of the room.

The majority of lights in Nova Scotia are rather of an inferior inexpensive description, and are not generally as good as those in other parts of the Dominion.
—Commissioner of Lights, 1871

This lamp was not part of the original apparatus. The light installed at Pomquet Island in 1868 consisted of four lamps. There was no magnifying lens, but there were twelve-inch concave (parabolic) metal reflectors to redirect the light from the flames. After the Commissioner of Lights complained in 1871 about the quality of Nova Scotia lights, a movement toward larger burners and reflectors began. While the new lamps used more oil, and thus were more expensive to maintain, the improvement in the lights far outweighed financial concerns.

By 1877 the Pomquet Island light station became the beneficiary of these improvements, and a circular burner lamp with an eighteen-inch reflector was added. Its particular colour was probably achieved by placing a pane of red glass in front of the reflector, a practice that was introduced in Nova Scotia around 1871 with mixed reviews from mariners. For some lights, addition of the red glass made the colour distinction clearly visible at sea, but for others, the wooden frames that held the glass blocked too much light and made the beacons less brilliant than before.

By March of 1910, two duplex lamps, one dozen "ruby chimneys," and a 270-degree, fifth-order "French lens" were on their way to Pomquet Island. Some of these made up the apparatus George Millar was examining for the first time.

The type of kerosene George would use was developed in 1846 by Dr. Abraham Gesner, a physician from Cornwallis, Nova Scotia. By the 1860s this coal extract was meeting exacting federal government standards and was replacing whale and seal oils as the fuel of choice—not only in Canada, but around the world. But it wasn't until the early 1870s that storage problems in places like Pomquet Island were addressed. The old wooden barrels that worked for storing other oils were too permeable for kerosene, so light stations around Nova Scotia began receiving tanks of galvanized iron.

Leaky barrels explained the convention of storing fuel oil well away from light towers and dwellings. Lights like the one at Pomquet Island were made to hold enough oil for one night's burning. It was not uncommon for lighthouses to burn down due to lightning strikes or errant fuel and flames. Fire safety, then, was a serious matter. Very early in his tenure, George Millar would establish a procedure whereby any spilled kerosene was immediately mopped up and wiped away with soap and water.

It would later become part of the Millars' annual routine to take delivery of roughly 140 gallons of kerosene in large barrels every July. The kerosene would come from a federal government ship that would anchor offshore and send supplies to the island in smaller craft called

As it is almost impossible to make and prepare oil barrels which will hold petroleum oil without leaking, a supply of these tanks to the lighthouses became essentially necessary as a matter of economy; and it is probable the saving of oil which will be effected thereby will soon pay for the tanks.
—Commissioner of Lights, 1871

tenders. Along with the fuel came such lighthouse necessities as rags for cleaning and polishing the light, whitewash and paint for the buildings and floors, logbooks for the keeper, washing soda to help break down the hard island water, and Surprise brand soap. Other than these articles and a government-issue rowboat, George's employer made no effort to ease the way of life for the human inhabitants of this small island. The Millars' comfort—indeed their survival—would depend almost entirely on personal ingenuity.

In George and Ruth Millar's time, lightkeepers' situations varied from complete isolation and exposure to the worst nature could dish out—such as the "humane establishment" at storm-tossed Sable Island—to fine homes close to free-standing light towers along the scenic shores of mainland Nova Scotia and Cape Breton. Somewhere in a category between abject hardship and relative ease was Pomquet Island. This small formation of land was often enveloped in fog or wracked by winds, and the six Millar children would always be conscious of isolation from their peers. There was no electricity and no running water. For their entire tenure, the Millars obtained drinking water by lowering a bucket on a length of rope into an eight-foot well, then drawing it hand over hand back to the surface. The well was marked only by a wooden platform with a hole just large enough to pass a bucket through. A lid covered this hole when it was not in use. Small children were warned to stay away, and as a result, it was George who usually fetched drinking water. Day in and day out, through rain, sleet, driving snow, and wind, George would bring the family fresh water using the only means of transport available: two legs, two feet, and a bucket.

The well water was too hard for washing clothes and hair, so tall wooden barrels called puncheons were stationed outside the house to catch rainwater from the eavestroughs. While it contained fewer minerals than the well water, even the rainwater required washing soda to soften it, and sea spray made it too salty for drinking. Since the puncheons froze in winter, melted snow sometimes took the place of rainwater for washing during cold weather, although it took ten inches of snow to yield just one inch of water. It went without saying that water was never wasted.

Some thirteen years after the Millars arrived on the island, a cistern was installed in the cellar that could collect and supply water for washing year-round and deliver it to the kitchen sink with the aid of a hand pump. But indoor plumbing did not advance past this innovation. The well remained the only source of drinking water, and the family made do with either chamber pots—"thunder jugs" to the men—or the outhouse. Early in his family's lightkeeping life, George upgraded the outhouse to a "two-holer": one large hole for the adults and a smaller one with a step for the children. The walls were decorated with the requisite illustrations from expired calendars and the tissue consisted of newspaper—preferred for its relative softness—and out-of-date catalogues from Simpson's, Eaton's, and Holman's of Prince Edward Island.

Still, there was comfort inside the home and a small measure of luxury that economic hardship accompanying the soon-to-come Great Depression did not allow some families on the mainland. For example, the Millars acquired a family car that was kept in a shed near the wharf at Bayfield, and they always had enough to eat. Sometimes the children took an extra lunch to school for their friends who weren't so fortunate. Over time, the family acquired a wind-up gramophone and a battery-powered radio. Especially on Sundays, mother, father, sisters, and brothers would gather around and listen to their favourite programs. George and Ruth also imported a pump organ, which had belonged to Ruth's long-deceased sister, and some fine china teacups handed down from Ruth's mother. These advantages, coupled with organ lessons and placemats, were some vestiges of proper Protestant convention that Ruth insisted upon keeping alive in her family. Lonely though their situation was, she was determined her children would not grow up with "oilcloth manners."

Transport of the organ to the island must have been an odyssey in itself. The instrument stood about five feet tall, extended almost six feet in length, and was referred to as a pump organ in an upright piano case. The wood of its exterior, which housed the bellows and reeds and movements that allowed sound to issue from its depths, was solid and thick, possibly walnut. It was finished darkly, and the wooden grillwork above the keyboard was backed with rich, red fabric. It was from behind this grill that sound came forth and on its lip that musical scores rested.

Every day Ruth would turn a key to unlock the smoothly curved lid that swung upward to reveal an ivory and ebony keyboard. Over the keys, the words "Goderich Organ Company" were stenciled in gold, and under these were the sundry stops that could be pushed in or pulled out to create variations in tone. The whole contraption was powered by two cast-iron foot pedals that were proclaimed "mouse proof" in bold relief on their front edges. A horse-hair-covered stool that stood on ornamented cast-iron legs swiveled up or down, depending upon the player's height. Ruth could be found on this stool daily, playing one tune after another, feet and knees pumping, fingers moving over the keys, looking rather like a swan: pedalling furiously underneath while the picture of serenity and competence on top. Rosa was the only one of Ruth's children to carry the legacy of her mother's organ lessons into adult life.

My mother played the organ. I can't remember her playing anything but hymns. She could play for an hour non-stop. The note one hymn would end on would be the first note of the next hymn!
—Rosa (Millar) Mattinson

Although the organ did not arrive on Pomquet Island immediately, there is no living memory of how it ultimately arrived, since the children were too young at the time to remember. However, there are only two possibilities: either it was ferried over on a scow in summer, or it was hauled on a sleigh over the ice in winter. It may have been easier to transport the massive and weighty instrument in winter because the movers would have been able to find an access point close to the house. Friction between burden and ground would have been less in winter, thus enabling one horse, with some help from his human friends, to haul the organ to the front yard. From there, it would have been a matter of wrestling the weighty instrument up the front steps and into the parlour.

As long as the Millars lived on Pomquet Island, the only means of hauling goods the half mile from the landing to the house were two wheel-less contraptions: one called a "drag" and the other a bobsled. The first was a sleigh-like contrivance of George's invention with wooden runners polished to a high gloss. The smooth polish was enough to reduce friction between drag and road so that a single horse could pull almost any load with reasonable ease. In winter, the large bobsled took the drag's place. It had two sets of runners—one fixed pair on the rear and one directional set on the front for steering. One of these sleds may have been pressed into service to deliver Ruth's organ.

A number of years after the Millar family took up residence on the island, George added a small luxury for himself—although it came in a roundabout way. With money he had earned fishing lobsters, George bought a small engine that he had intended to fit to the family rowboat. The new machine would roar to life without fail inside his homemade test drum, but whenever he fixed it to the boat and pushed off into the bay, the engine would refuse to start. After numerous attempts to launch, the family christened the Evinrude engine "Ever-rude" and sent it back. With the refund, George purchased a wind generator that he installed on the roof of the woodshed. Its main purpose was to charge the battery in the household radio, but an added bonus was that it could also power an electric light inside the woodshed. This allowed him to set up a small workshop where he

An annual event of great importance was the coming of the supply boat in summer. We never knew for sure which day it would come, but I think it usually arrived around mid-July. Huge oil tanks with enough kerosene to run the lamp in the light tower all year were the greatest load. Other things included paint, soap, and cleaning rags. (The tower was kept spotless!) We children stood at a safe distance and watched the proceedings with much interest.
—Thelma (Millar) Beairsto

could pursue the finer aspects of carpentry and mechanics in daylight and darkness alike.

Even with these adaptations, it remained a lifelong lighthouse fact that the only way to communicate with the mainland—either about daily affairs or in emergencies—was by getting into a boat and making the voyage to Bayfield wharf, or by walking across the ice in winter. Although many lightkeepers of the time had poles rigged to their light towers upon which could be hoisted distress flags, a similar apparatus was not an accessory at the Pomquet Island light. Even if it had been, there were many occasions when a flag could be no help at all. The first such time came soon enough.

When a woman's husband is at risk, she is conscious of it. It is part of the connection that holds them together. It is not quite the fine cord that binds a woman to her children and vibrates with all their cares, but it is a cord all the same.

So when the wind started to pick up on a September day in 1925 and the sky began to close in, Ruth thought of George. He had gone to the mainland early to do some business at the wharf, pick up the mail, and bring back the daily *Morning Chronicle* that he shared with David Sutton. Now it was lunchtime, and Ruth could see slate grey clouds rolling in over the hills of Cape Breton far to the east, and white caps whipping up across St. George's Bay.

All the while that she was nursing two-month-old Malcolm, and all the while that she was preparing and feeding lunch to Thelma and Rosa, Ruth was snatching glances through the back door of the kitchen toward the track from the landing. Only the increasingly swaying trees nodded to her. Malcolm fell asleep in her arms and the girls finished eating. Ruth tidied them up, put them all down for their naps, and washed the dishes. Still no George.

Ruth was not ordinarily prone to anxiety, but she was anxious now. George was supposed to be home an hour ago and punctuality was a trait he valued highly. She tiptoed upstairs and peeked in on Rosa and

Thelma sound asleep in their small beds. There would be no harm in running down to the landing just to see if George might be trying to get a message to her from the other side. Ruth took an extra blanket and scooped up a still-sleeping Malcolm. Ignoring coat and boots, she hurried down the track with her bundle and reached the landing in good time, breathless, hair astray from the wind.

"There he is!"

The wind was whipping stronger now, and whitecaps studded the quarter mile between breakwater and landing. Small waves lashed at the rocks along the shore and the clouds continued to bear down, heavier now, darker, lower. Across the water, George raised his arm in a wide arc to let Ruth know he'd seen her.

"Good. Everything's fine."

She hugged Malcolm tighter to shield them both from the rapidly cooling wind and felt the first tentative drops of rain strike her bare arms. Meanwhile, George clambered down the rip-rap of the breakwater, untied his rowboat, and pushed off.

Then it came: a wall of rain pressing across the bay, whipping up wind and waves in front of it, pelting down so hard the drops sounded like a waterfall on the surface of the sea. Cape Breton wasn't visible any more. She had only turned away for an instant, but now the breakwater wasn't visible either.

"Oh, dear Lord, keep Hubby safe!" prayed Ruth. She strained for a sight of George but could see nothing but driving rain.

She was already soaked and Malcolm was going to be next. George was on his way and there was nothing she could do now to help him. The best thing would be to get back to the house before the baby caught a chill and the children woke from their naps.

Ruth half-jogged, half-walked back to the lighthouse. Her arms were wrapped tightly around the blanketed baby and her head was bent to the track in front of her. Words George had said in jest a while back wouldn't stay out of her mind: "If I get lost at sea, you'll have to look after the light yourself." He had been grinning at her over the glowing red lens, and Ruth had scolded him for making light of something so serious. Now the import of his words was sinking in.

What will I do here with three babies and no boat? I can't even swim!

Pull yourself together, girl, and wait. No sense getting yourself all in a stew about nothing. Wait for George to get home.

It was her father's no-nonsense voice echoing inside her head and it calmed her somewhat. But George didn't come home—not in the forty minutes that it would normally take from the breakwater to the house, not in an hour.

"Maybe he turned back when the wind came up. That's probably what he did." Ruth kept telling herself this all day and all night. It was the only way she could keep George's words out of her mind.

The girls were pleased to have their mother playing games with them through the afternoon, something she didn't usually take time to do. At supper, Thelma asked, "Where's Daddy?" and Ruth answered as evenly as she could, "He's staying on the mainland for the night."

Still, she entreated her little daughters to add an extra prayer for Daddy to come safely home before she tucked them away to sleep.

At dusk, Ruth lit the lighthouse lamp and scanned the dark sea. For what, she could not say. Even if George did capsize or lose his oars and go adrift, she would not be able to see him now, not be able to help him even if she did. In bed, Ruth couldn't sleep. They'd never spent a night of their marriage apart, and the feather tick gaped widely on the side where George usually lay.

By dawn, Ruth could hear the rain letting up. The wail of the wind had stopped, and by the time she extinguished the lighthouse lamp there was only a soft rain falling. She moved to close the drapes of the lantern house but lingered for a few moments to bore her eyes as far as she could into the track from the landing. *If I look for long enough maybe he'll appear.*

Sure enough, there was George, trudging damply through the trees in the early light.

He had been aiming for noon, as he'd told Ruth when he left the morning before. But he got held up at the wharf, first helping untangle some nets, then arguing the price of lobster with Fred Irving, the cannery owner. When the squall hit, George had been only a few strokes from the breakwater in a boat that had been supplied the previous summer by the Department of Marine and Fisheries. As small breakers began to broadside the craft and the boat began to rock almost uncontrollably, George remembered what old Mr. Murphy had said when the thing was delivered.

"You'd be better off to put that to use as kindlin', George. She's not goin' ta carry you across this harbour."

It was all George could do to get the craft turned around and back to the breakwater without rolling over. Sputtering and wet, he jogged to the lobster cannery. There, the manager had a shack where he did business and sometimes slept overnight. George spent the afternoon and night there before striking out again at first light.

The first thing he did at home after changing into dry clothes and filling himself with a hot breakfast was to start composing a letter. He and Ruth spent the weekend crafting the words to a point which they judged showed sufficient respect, yet conveyed George's justifiable indignation. Then, they pulled out the lined Department of Marine and Fisheries memo paper, followed the printed instructions ("Only one subject to be referred to in one letter; write on one side of the paper only") and penned George's first official complaint:

September 28th, 1925
Agent
Dep't of Marine
Chtwn, P.E.I.

Sir:
I feel that I am now fully justified in making a complaint about the boat that was left here for me a year ago by the 'supply boat.' The craft

never suited me from the very first, as I consider that it is very unsuited for this place and she has no more bottom or bearance to her that [sic] a canoe, a person has to keep their head still and hold their breath when aboard her. I never used her much last season, as I have a boat of my own. But this season I have been forced into using her on account of my own being up for repairs.

Last Friday capped the climax, when a sudden squall came up when I was on the main land and in trying to get back to the Island, I all but drowned myself.

This boat was condemned by the "old keeper" from the very first sight, and I am now fully convinced that he knew what he was talking about. Trust you will give this matter your attention, as I must have a good sea-worthy craft here.

Yours truly,
G.E. Millar (keeper)

George was not the first to complain to his superiors about a standard-issue craft. In an 1875 report to the Minister of Marine and Fisheries, the Nova Scotia lighthouse agent noted that Pomquet Island's first keeper, John Atwater, complained his boat was "somewhat out of repair" and that, at seventeen feet long, was too large to be managed by one person. The agent recommended that Atwater be supplied, not only with a new boat, but a boathouse as well. The building never did materialize, and it was 1893 before the next report came of a new boat for the island.

George Millar's urgent request did not go unheeded by his superiors, but neither was it granted with lightning speed. Still, there did not appear to be a complaint about the time frame of the boat replacement project in George's next memo of January 1, 1927:

Mr. W. H. Prowse
Sup't. of Lights
Ch'twn, P.E.I.

Sir:

In reply to your letter of the 27th [indecipherable word]. Regarding measurements for the row-boat I require.

I have endeavoured by the accompanying sketch to convey something of what I require, by way of dimensions.

While not drawn to scale, it will no doubt give something of the idea of what I want. These measurements are taken from a very good boat, and if you bring me one after her mode[l] I will have no cause to complain.

But in placing an order for this boat, I wi[sh] you to impress it on the builders mind, that she, must be <u>light</u>, <u>shoal</u> in draught, and <u>stiff</u>, flat-bottomed not rounded like a cigar.

Yours very truly,
G.E. Millar

Accompanying this memo were two drawings of a proposed row-boat, one a top view and one a side view. The suggested dimensions were for an overall length of fourteen feet.

Eventually, a boat was supplied that served the Millar family satisfactorily. Still absent a boathouse, George erected a windlass that, by means of a hand crank and some rope, could haul a craft out of the water. This convenience made things easier on George and also saved the more lightweight members of the family from getting their feet wet before entering the boat. In later years, the family fleet consisted of three vessels, each with its own purpose. There was a lobster boat (The *Vimy R*) powered by a single-cylinder gas engine known as a "one-lunger." There was also a smaller boat fitted with a canvas spray hood that could be powered by the same engine and used during the summer to ferry the family back and forth to the mainland. Lastly, a three-person rowboat would be pressed into service as the fall weather became cooler and the water became rougher. This was likely the government-issued craft.

Still, there was no getting around the fact that wind, weather, and ice could foil any voyage at any time. This lent a constant element of risk and isolation to life on Pomquet Island. But George and Ruth shared a strong faith and inborn ingenuity that equipped them for survival. They would pass this sense of sturdy self-reliance on to their children—even if Ruth never did learn how to swim.

*The second summer we were on the island we had a visit
from the stork…I had left my wife in the capable hands
of a practical nurse, Mrs. Chisholm…Then I went to the
mainland to phone the doctor and wait to ferry him over.*
— George Millar

The Stork

CHAPTER THREE

"Now, Thelma and Rosa…" Mrs. Chisholm knelt to bring her sure gaze level with the eyes of the two small sisters, one warm and ample hand on each child's shoulder. "Why don't you both go down to the landing and watch for your daddy? He'll be coming along soon with Dr. MacDonald."

"Why is he coming with the doctor?" asked Thelma, just three-and-a-half years old.

"The doctor is going to help us after the stork comes," answered the midwife in the calm, smiling way that makes children feel their lives are in the best of care.

"Stork?" Rosa—not quite two—knew that word.

"Yes." Mrs. Chisholm brought her face closer to the two small girls and lowered her voice just a bit. "He's bringing a new baby!"

Rosa and Thelma didn't know much about storks, but they had often seen the tall, blue birds that came almost every day to wade on giant matchstick legs in the shallow waters around their island. They knew the birds could stand on one great leg for what seemed like hours at a time. Daddy called them cranes—sometimes storks—and told his daughters the birds were fishing. This image gave Thelma trouble. It had flashed in her mind as soon as Mrs. Chisholm said "stork." What did fishing have to do with a new baby? And where was Mumma?

Over her shoulder, Mrs. Chisholm was conscious of Ruth Millar in the downstairs bedroom ready to give birth any minute. There wasn't time for small talk, and there wasn't time for the doctor to get there. She had known this when she sent George off four hours ago to find a telephone and to wait for the doctor at the wharf. It would be best if the girls, too, weren't in the house when the baby arrived.

Mrs. Chisholm had presided over many home births—including those of the two tots now before her. She didn't rattle easily. It gave her pleasure to usher in additions to the young families in her charge. She had arrived on Pomquet Island a few days before in order to be present when the baby was born, and she had been glad to make the trip. Still, these were unusual circumstances: no running water, no electricity, no telephone, and no neighbours to call upon in difficulty. Even though doctors in these parts were mostly a formality during births, one could never be too sure about complications. It was always wise to have a physician at least on the way as the baby was born. But now it was almost one o'clock in the afternoon, which meant Dr. MacDonald must have been occupied with another patient when George had tried to get through. Who knew when the good doctor would have received George's message, and who knew where the doctor might have been when he received it? Even after all of that, there was the two-hour jostle over clay roads between the practice in Antigonish and Bayfield wharf. As she glanced at her watch, the midwife knew this birth was being left to her and the Man Upstairs.

"Is Daddy gone fishing for a baby?" Thelma was still trying to understand how a baby, a bird, and her father could all be connected.

Mrs. Chisholm didn't want to get started down that road, so she was casting about for a way to avoid Thelma's question when the teacups in the pantry caught her eye. She stood and reached beyond Rosa to a shelf high above the toddler's head, from which she scooped two cups. She thrust one at each of the sisters. "Why don't you pick some blueberries on the way to meet your father?"

The girls accepted the cups carefully, with both hands, and examined them closely. Before either could say another word, Mrs. Chisholm was herding them from the summer kitchen, through the porch, and out the rear door. "Now you run along, girls, and be sure to bring your Daddy back with you."

"But…" began Thelma, gingerly holding a delicately flowered cup and turning her round, blue eyes to the older woman. The door latch snapped firmly in front of the child, and Thelma watched Mrs. Chisholm's back disappear beyond the imperfect lens of the screen door. It was too late to go back inside. The orders had been given.

"But we're not…" Thelma trailed off, with only Rosa to concur.

It was a fine summer day, so the midwife was confident the children would have lots to keep them busy. She had been thinking they would pick blueberries, but as she stepped into the bedroom she remembered: blueberries wouldn't be ready for picking yet. Oh, well—strawberries, then. This was her first visit to the island, so Mrs. Chisholm didn't realize the only place for the children to find wild strawberries was a patch a hundred paces or so from the front vestibule, near the cliff's edge. In the back of her mind she did worry about a three-and-a-half-year-old and a two-year-old outside on an island with high cliffs, large rocks, and water everywhere, but right now, there were more urgent matters to attend to. Mrs. Chisholm wouldn't bring up the subject of the children if Ruth didn't ask.

Outside, the little girls were communing in solemn silence over what to do with their mother's precious teacups. At their age, they didn't retain much, but this they did know: They would never have been allowed even to carry their mother's fine china, let alone use it for picking berries. Mrs. Chisholm was either ignorant of this fact or unconcerned by it. Still, she was a grown-up and, therefore, was to be obeyed. The sisters were on the horns of a dilemma. Mumma would know what to do, but where was Mumma?

Just then a blue jay buzzed by, calling as he went, and dove into a spruce tree just a few yards away. It was enough to break the earnest ruminations. "Let's go this way." Thelma began to move in the bird's direction toward the shady red path that led through the trees to the landing. On the way, there would be lots of blueberry bushes.

It was in a clump of these bushes that George and Dr. MacDonald found Thelma and Rosa an hour later. Too far away from the strawberry plants to seek them out, and finding it too early for ripe blueberries, the pair had made themselves busy tracking bugs and beetles as they wove up and down through the twiggy undergrowth. The china cups were still intact but lying empty and forgotten on the grass beside the track.

"Did you catch a baby?" Thelma was hurrying to stay in step beside her father while he walked as briskly as he could with Rosa on his hip.

"Wait and see." George's tone did not encourage follow-up questions.

George reached out and took Thelma's hand to help his oldest daughter keep up. Dr. MacDonald walked ahead with his black leather bag in one hand and the two china cups in the other. When this odd party arrived at the house, the two small sisters were left outside until George and the doctor could ascertain the conditions indoors. True to Mrs. Chisholm's judgment, the baby had been born before the two men arrived on the scene. It was July 14, 1925, and Malcolm would be the only one of the Millar children born on Pomquet Island.

Two sisters and one more brother followed over the next ten years, but each of these children was born in the hospital on the mainland and brought back home only after mother and child were certified fit to make the trip. Although Ruth's trips to town were planned months in advance, the children weren't kept abreast of all that was happening.

In February of 1929, for example, Ruth made a visit to a friend in Antigonish—or at least, that was what she told her family—leaving George on the island with the three children. She stayed away for a few weeks, returning with a new baby girl. This child was named Minna Elizabeth in acknowledgement of her grandmothers, Minnie Mitchell and Elizabeth Millar.

Two winters later, in 1931, the entire family moved to the mainland, where they occupied a newly constructed house while its generous builder, James Randall, occupied a shed in the yard. Not all of the blankets went on beds that winter. Some were used to stop holes in the unfinished walls. Even though the spare bedding was not effective at keeping in the heat, it at least kept out the snow. In February of that year, Ruth made another prolonged visit to Antigonish and, again, she came home with a baby, a boy this time. He

When it became apparent that the Stork was going to win out in the race, Mrs. Chisholm said to my wife, "Don't worry, everything will be all right. The Lord is here and He'll look after us." How right she was! As the doctor and I entered the kitchen, there was Mrs. Chisholm calmly bathing my son Malcolm.
—George Millar

was named David after his maternal grandfather and given the second name, James, after his paternal grandfather.

There was one luxury that came with Ruth's absences, though. It was the bread. While she was away, Thelma and Rosa would be delegated the task of mixing the dough and setting it in a pan atop the warming oven to let it rise. When the pale dough could be seen, soft and spongy, inching above the sides of the bread pan, it was time for their father to intervene. George had the strength to knead the dough, and the bread that he worked always had a sumptuous texture that even their mother could not achieve.

Just after Christmas in 1934, George was knitting new heads for his lobster traps one evening near the range in the lighthouse dining room.

The children were gathered around the table under the bright kerosene light of the Aladdin lamp. They were busy with games and reading, while their mother—who had been getting plump of late—kept her own spot within the circle of light mending socks. Just then, Rosa heard their father say, "I suppose I'll spend quite a bit of time like this while you're in town next month."

Rosa's heart sank. Visits to town always seemed to mean new babies and new chores for she and Thelma. Her deductive logic proved correct: a baby sister, Barbara Jean, was added to the family on January 31, 1935. It was an especially cold winter that year, so when Barbara arrived from Antigonish, she was privileged to be driven all the way to the front door of the Pomquet Island lighthouse. The ice was solid enough, and the track on the island clear enough, that George was able to drive his car all the way home.

I wasn't pleased with the idea, for that meant diapers, diapers that Thelma and I would have to wash and hang out on the line—not a pleasant prospect to an eleven-year-old at any time, much less in winter.
—Rosa (Millar) Mattinson

The changeable ice between island and mainland rarely allowed this much luxury. There were times when ice and water behaved like co-conspirators trying to swallow up all who would pass over them, and there were times when the winter winds seemed bent on using these cruel players to cut the family off from help when it was needed most. In the winter of 1933, these spiteful forces of nature almost succeeded.

Ruth didn't know what to do, and it was an unfamiliar feeling. She was standing in the dining room—kitchen, really, now that it was winter—watching but not seeing Rosa and Thelma preparing the noon table for dinner. Two-year-old David had been sick for almost a week. Ruth and George had no instrument to measure his fever, but they knew it was high. His colour and the feel of his brow told them that. So they brought his crib downstairs to the parlour, where it would be out of the drafts and coddled by heat from the pot-bellied coal stove. The stove would now be fed constantly from the preciously small store of coal in the cellar.

Ruth had done everything a mother could do. She had wrapped her baby up to keep him warm, she had bathed him in wet rags to cool him down, she had held him and walked with him while he coughed, and she had patted his back to loosen the phlegm. Most of all, she had prayed. She was almost ready to try a mustard plaster, although she knew the toddler's skin would be too tender to bear it. Maybe it was time to send for the doctor.

When Ruth called George in for his midday meal, she waited by the back door to meet him. As he entered, he brought with him a rush of fresh winter air. Ruth crossed her arms and gave him room as he stamped the January snow off his boots and brushed some errant wood chips from his arms and shoulders. Ruth's customary smile for her husband was absent. "The baby's getting worse. I think we'd better call for the doctor."

George was stepping into the unheated summer kitchen, skinning off his winter cap as he went and shaking fresh snow from it. "Are you sure? I thought he looked not too bad this morning."

He hung the cap on its hook, then bent over to unlace his knee-high winter boots. As he did, his voice took on a stooped-over timbre. "Why don't we wait and see how he is in the morning?"

He was thinking that bringing the doctor from Antigonish all the way out here to the ends of the earth in the middle of winter was not something to be done without a good reason. What if the doctor got waylaid here and missed an emergency on the mainland? Still working on his boots, George caught a glimpse of Ruth through a frame made by his legs and the hem of his winter mackinaw. It flashed in his mind that, even from upside down, she seemed to be using her arms to hold herself in.

"No, we'll not wait."

Ruth didn't feel the cold of the unused room as she watched her husband straighten up, shake snow from his winter coat, and hang it on a hook next to his hat. "I'd like you to go over to the mainland right after dinner and call Dr. McMaster."

Ruth didn't usually take that tone with her husband, but she knew what waiting had done decades ago for her older sister. She didn't have one anymore. There'd be no "wait to see if it gets better" this time. They'd waited long enough.

At her words, George stopped what he was doing and turned around, one hand still on the coat hook. He looked at his wife, taking care this time to really see her. She had a curiously unkempt air about her, despite her hair drawn taut to the back of her head as always (she could make that bun in her sleep) and despite the clean, printed house dress that looked just as neat and trim as all the others. George couldn't put his finger on it, but there was something in her face or in her bearing that said her always-present self-control was slipping.

He kicked his boots into the corner. In his thick wool socks with pant legs tucked in, snow cakes still clinging to the tops, George strode across the summer kitchen, through the dining room, past his other children seated at the table, and into the parlour to take another look at his youngest son. It was plain to George that the boy was struggling to breathe, even in his sleep. He looked hot despite the cooling cloth on his forehead. Ruth was right. He was getting worse.

"All right." George put his arm lightly around Ruth's waist as she joined him at the crib. "I'll go to the mainland to phone the doctor as soon as I finish dinner."

David showed no improvement when George looked in on him the next morning before heading for the wharf to meet Dr. McMaster, a young physician who had replaced the ageing Dr. MacDonald a few years earlier. As he rowed across a harbour still clear of ice, he was privately glad he'd bowed to his wife's insistence the day before. He was thankful that yesterday's light snowfall had stopped and it was a good day for travel.

Once the physician arrived in the sick room a few hours later, it didn't take him long to assess the damage. "Mr. and Mrs. Millar, your boy has a well-developed case of pneumonia."

Ruth and George were standing together, facing the doctor from the opposite side of the crib. They had watched intently as he moved his stethoscope around little David's rib cage—first the front, then the back. He moved quickly, not needing to stop the round instrument long in one spot to find what he was listening for.

"His lungs are filling up. I'll give him some quinine to help with the fever and infection, but I think I ought to send a nurse, too."

George and Ruth did not need to confer on this one. They nodded their heads in unison.

"I know it'll be expensive, George, but he needs watching—vigilance, really—around the clock. You and Mrs. Millar can't do it by yourselves, and the others are too young for a job this important."

The two men made the arrangements when they got back to the mainland, and George was at the wharf the next morning to pick up Nurse Chisholm. George had been envisioning someone like the older Mrs. Chisholm, the midwife, so he wasn't too impressed by what he first saw: there on the wharf was a slip of a girl set against a grey sky that was heavy with coming snow. She was shivering from foot to foot on the cold planks and looked to George like one of those people who didn't know how to dress for the weather. Her thin camel-hair coat, cocky brown tam and store-bought gloves would be no match for the weather on Pomquet Island. She would find that out on the walk between the landing and the house.

This young lady would be lucky not to catch pneumonia herself, let alone nurse someone who already had it. Something in the senior Chisholm's thick frame and copious proportions—along with a few strands of grey hair—gave George confidence in her ability. This nurse was young, George's junior by perhaps a decade or so, and she hadn't yet assumed the air of competence that people develop after they've been doing the same thing for a long time. Still, George reassured himself, she had book learning and she was a registered nurse. This kept her up with the changing world, supposedly, but it didn't mean she was a better healer than the older midwife. Even a shared surname didn't mean her elder's knack for nursing had been passed on.

"So you're the nurse, are you?"

George's tone had a dryness to it that the young woman was not too obtuse to catch. She watched him fold the oars into the boat and grab at the timbers of the wharf to bring himself alongside so he could tie up.

"Yes, I am."

The words came rather too brightly for the heavy cold of this January day. Still, she didn't flinch when she bent toward the boat to hand down her bag of belongings for George to secure under the seat in the bow. This was because it wasn't the nurse's first time in a rowboat, and that was a mark in her favour. Without prompting, she climbed right down the ladder and smoothly—without being told—took her seat at the stern without causing so much as a sway.

"Looks like snow."

They were away from the wharf now, and the words seemed to push out of George as he pulled on the oars. Miss Chisholm met his dark stare from her hard, wooden perch. She sat neatly, feet together, purse on her lap.

"Yes it does." She was trying to stay buoyant, but it was difficult under the weight of George's mood and the pregnant sky.

It was a quiet trip. The nurse didn't need to ask questions. She had already learned the details of David's illness from the doctor when they spoke the day before. She picked up quickly enough that George wasn't interested in idle chatter, particularly on this day.

The snow began just about the time George and a discretely shivering Nurse Chisholm arrived at the lighthouse. Through the night the wind picked up, the temperature plummeted, and ice began to form in the harbour. With the water not completely frozen, there would be no walking to the mainland. But, with the water not completely clear, there would be no rowing either. In fact, there would be no more travel to the mainland for two weeks. Medical help had come in the nick of time.

George's predecessor had warned him not to get caught in "the lolly." Lolly, or frazil, was the part-ice, part-slush that often started to form in early winter. While it seemed harmless enough on approach, the farther in you took your boat, the faster you were stuck. Once surrounded by lolly, there would be no going forward and no retreating, only waiting until it decided to let you go. So the Millar family's boats waited at the landing, gathering their own shrouds of snow while winter came on and navigation in St. George's Bay ceased for another season.

Travel was not going to matter to Miss Chisholm anyway, because she was needed every day of the next two weeks. David's sickness didn't want to let go, and the house was becoming more and more subdued as the gravity of the situation settled on the other children. Ruth and George were going through the motions of life as usual, but even the children could see that they were starting to wear down. In spite of having a nurse around to help, there wasn't much anyone could do to make the boy breathe easier. The air whistled through his nose or rattled in his lungs almost every time he inhaled, and the heave of his chest that came with every intake of breath made even his watchers struggle to draw more air. It was a dismal time.

But just as quickly as hope can be taken away, it can be given back. George was in the barn with the animals, and the older children were occupied with school work at the dining room table. Four-year-old Minna "helped" with her own paper and pencil. They were all conscious of Nurse Chisholm pacing the parlour floor with David in her arms. Each time the nurse passed the opening to the dining room, the creak of the floor boards reminded them that she was there—as if Ruth needed reminding that her baby was so sick she was unable to do all the nursing herself.

But today was Ruth's day to churn butter. The cream had reached the desired temperature of seventy-two degrees Fahrenheit in its tall crockery churn behind the stove, so Ruth brought it out and began her work. The slow steady motion of lifting and pushing the wooden dash into the cream was a comfort somehow. As she worked, there was a rhythmic swish from the liquid, muffled inside its earthen chamber. At least this was a constant. It reminded her of pleasant times, so she allowed her mind to drift.

After about fifteen minutes, Ruth could feel the cream beginning to thicken. Some of her tension was releasing now, even though she kept having to push and pull harder with each movement of the dash. This was the crucial time, as the cream separated into butter and watery buttermilk. At the right moment, she would take the new butter out of the churn and wash it before salting it and pressing it into moulds. This would be a good-sized batch, so she would stamp it "G. M." before putting it down in the cellar. The initials would identify it just in case some might later go to Charlie Gass at the general store in return for groceries. It was usually worth about six cents a pound.

Absorbing as this work may have been, Ruth still hadn't found enough steadiness to keep from jumping just a bit when she felt a gentle hand on her shoulder. It was Nurse Chisholm—"Chizzie" to the children by now.

"I'll finish the churning, Mrs. Millar. You should go to the baby. He needs you."

It took a split second for Ruth to return to the present. "But it's just starting to set."

Her eyes moved from the churn to the nurse, and she recognized the urgency in the other's eyes as she repeated, "I'll finish the churning. The baby is very sick. You should go to him."

Only the older sisters, aged twelve and ten, caught the significance of this tableau. They looked on while Ruth and Chizzie regarded each other over the churn at the opposite end of the dining room table. Thelma and Rosa watched their mother wordlessly press the handle of the dash forward into the nurse's hands, then move into the parlour, eyes fixed the whole time on the crib in a dark corner. They watched her scoop David into her arms and begin the familiar pacing. His small arms and legs appeared to be flailing now, and his wheeze was loud enough to be heard clearly, even above the steady plop and squish of butter-making. Nurse Chisholm seemed to have her attention riveted on the churn with her back turned purposely toward the parlour.

No one said a word. Even Minna sat quietly in her chair, where she had only moments ago been chattily drawing a picture of the family horse, Jumbo, for Malcolm to see. The parlour floorboards creaked as Ruth paced, her head bent so close to her son's that it was difficult to see her face. David moved in sporadic kicks as though trying to throw off the blanket of sickness that was smothering him. Then he went quiet.

There was no more movement in the child's arms and legs. David's siblings at the dining table could no longer hear his breathing. Ruth waited, poised mid-step, her back to the table, ready to keep walking with him as soon as his struggle resumed. But it didn't resume—not in two minutes, not in three.

Finally, Ruth turned her head and called over her shoulder for Nurse Chisholm: "You'd better come and have a look." Her voice was weighty but it was sure, much the same as it would have been had David been a sick calf and the nurse been George.

By now all of the other children were holding their breath. They saw their mother hand the child over to Chizzie, and they watched as Chizzie lay him down in the crib. She examined him with her stethoscope. Then she looked up to Ruth and spoke softly. "The crisis is passed. He should be better now."

The other children didn't realize they had not been breathing until that moment. They let go a collective sigh but were still too raptly intent on their mother's back to speak. They saw her shoulders drop just a little and a hand go to her face. The fingers of the other hand touched the back of her head, checking that all her hairpins were in place before moving lower, to the back of her neck, where she let them rest for a moment. Miss Chisholm was still bent over David as Ruth spun around, handkerchief to her nose, and strode to the back door to call George in with the news.

As she passed her two eldest, she remembered: "Rosa and Thelma, you'd better finish the churning and get the butter into blocks before it spoils." They noticed that their mother's voice had taken on a half-muffled, nasal quality behind the handkerchief, but it was plenty strong by the time she opened the back door. "George! George! Come in and see. The baby's better!"

The oldest sisters had been given the job of finishing the butter many times before, so they knew what to do: Thelma started taking the top off the churn while Rosa fetched the washing pan from the pantry. Their mother brushed by them again—this time heading in the opposite direction—as if her daughters were invisible.

A few moments later, George was stamping into the summer kitchen porch. The children expected to see him pause at least to unlace his boots and kick them off, but he didn't even do that before breezing through the dining room and into the parlour. He left tread prints of snow on the floor and brought the cold through with him, but neither Ruth nor Miss Chisholm complained of that when he arrived at the side of David's crib.

For a moment he said nothing, observing his son's peaceful slumber. Then a slow smile spread from underneath his thick moustache to his eyes, and he turned to the nurse. "I guess it's a good thing we brought you over when we did. One more day and we'd have been left out here on our own."

These words were all that was needed. The children could speak and get on with their occupations again. Life was back to normal and all was right with the world.

It wasn't long before the weather began to clear. A few days later, when everyone was sure the crisis had passed, Nurse Chisholm bundled up in her pretty city coat and hat and threw around her neck a freshly knit scarf that was a gift from the family. George, who would pull the bags on a hand sleigh, led the young nurse on a brisk walk across the ice to the mainland. In time, David would make a complete recovery, although his wobbly toddler's legs would have to be trained to walk all over again, and his chest would be his weak spot for many years to come. Nurse Chisholm was satisfied she'd earned George's respect for her efforts, and she knew his gratitude was deeper than the words he managed to get out as he left her at the train station.

"Thank you. Thank you for everything."

A day at school entailed a walk of three miles…a short trip by boat, and the same procedure at the end of the day. So my wife saw to it that, before any of the children began to attend the local school, they had an introduction and speaking acquaintance with the Three R's.

—George Millar

Acquaintance with the Three R's

CHAPTER FOUR

George Millar's love wasn't in what he said to his children, it was in what he did for them. And what gave him the most pride was making sure each of them received a grade twelve education. It may have been that his own father-in-law did not believe in "educatin' women" and had denied Ruth's wish to become a teacher, and it may have been that George himself demanded his wife's acquiescence in most matters. Nevertheless, among his children, the girls would have the same opportunities as the boys. They all would graduate from grade twelve, no small accomplishment for a large family living on an island in rural Nova Scotia during the Great Depression.

Perhaps it was George's own thirst for knowledge that fueled his ambition. Having ended his own formal education in grade eight, he took pride in the things he continued to learn on his own, and he would sometimes use chores around the home to demonstrate the value of formal schooling.

In these endeavours, George was supported wholeheartedly by his wife. Ruth's childhood dream of being a teacher was never realized in the formal sense, but she was a teacher to each of her six children.

Rosa and Thelma both started school in 1928, despite a twenty-one-month age difference. Rosa had turned five in August and Thelma would be seven in December. Their mother had been preparing them for this day, teaching them how to read and count. They had enjoyed trying their new skills and showing their parents how smart they were. Ruth had worked for weeks during her spare time at the treadle sewing machine, crafting twin jumpers and bloomers out of new, red-and-tan gingham that the sisters would wear on their first day of school.

After a session on the end of the Swede saw helping him cut firewood, he'd say, "Are you going to do your lessons now or do you want to grow up to be a pick-and-shovel man?"
—*Malcolm Millar*

It was a clear September day when George drove Thelma and Rosa to the Bayfield schoolhouse, which sat on a hill overlooking the water. They could see Pomquet Island in the distance as they tumbled from George's Model A Ford into the dusty schoolyard, eager to begin. There was excitement in the air, and children were everywhere. Briefly, the schoolyard chatter quieted as Rosa and Thelma eyed their would-be friends. Even though this was a first meeting for most of them, all the mainland children knew who these girls were. Miss MacKinnon had been apprised of their academic progress and was expecting them. The sisters saw George disappear inside the one-room schoolhouse for a few minutes, then re-emerge to climb back into the car. Thelma and Rosa remained rooted to their spots on the school's front step.

George leaned out the car window toward them before he drove away. "Be at the end of the breakwater by four o'clock and I'll be there with the boat to take you home." He ducked inside, ground the gear shift into reverse, then sloped a shoulder out the window one more time. "Don't be late."

What he didn't tell them was that Thelma would be starting grade two and Rosa would be put in grade one. Back on Pomquet Island, Rosa and Thelma had been equals, always in each other's company, learning and doing similar things, sharing the same responsibilities. But on this day, all of that changed. Rosa could not understand how she was qualified only for grade one while her older sister was allowed to start farther ahead in grade two. Rosa wondered what she had done to be held back. It didn't seem fair. But her respect-your-elders training had been too well learned. She did not ask anyone why—not Miss MacKinnon, not her mother, and certainly not her father.

But it was a long and tiring walk from the school back to the wharf twice a day, too long and too tiring for one little girl to undertake on her own. Neither of the sisters would have thought of this, taking each other's company for granted as they did. George and Ruth had considered it, though, which is why they decided Thelma should wait to start school until Rosa was old enough to walk with her—even if the younger girl was barely old enough to start grade one and the older one long past the starting age.

The other thing George hadn't told the two new scholars was that there would be no more drives to school after that first day. From now on, they would be expected to make the three-mile hike between the breakwater and the school twice a day. And they were expected to be on time. For a time in that first year, Rosa was taken back home for schooling because her small legs were no match for the arduous walk, first to the landing on the island, then along the breakwater, then along the up-and-down dirt road to the school. Rosa's disposition toward illness had already earned from George a nickname, "the cold susceptible," so being kept at home was another troubling signal from her parents that, somehow, she did not quite measure up.

Then came the day that George himself did not make the crossing to pick up his daughters. One November morning the weather had started out fine enough, but by the time school let out, there was a gale blowing from the northeast. Thelma and Rosa set out as usual for their return walk down the long road toward the breakwater. Much of the trip was fun because the wind was at their backs. The big gusts could make them run faster and throw things farther. But as they turned off the main road for the last mile to their pick-up point, the blast caught them almost head-on.

They were too busy at first—struggling to hold their school books, keeping their coats together, and pushing against the gale—to see Ella Mae Grant fall into step beside them. She was one of the big girls who'd already left school, and she lived with her mother nearby. Ella Mae had manoeuvred herself in front of the youngsters and turned around to face them in order to keep her words from being blown away on the wind.

"Your father probably won't be picking you up today, girls!"

She was wearing a too-small sweater over her house dress, which was blowing wildly against her legs. She had one hand on her forehead to keep her hair from blowing in her eyes and one tight to her body holding her sweater together.

"Yes he will!" Thelma was sure of that. "He always does!" She had to shout with all her might, even though she had been taught never to shout at adults.

Ella Mae shook her head vigorously and strained her own voice. "Not today! It's too windy!" She waved an arm roughly in the direction of the bay. "Water's too rough!"

Rosa didn't believe Ella Mae either. Her father was master of everything. "Of course he'll be there!" She clutched her school bag to her chest. Knowing that the headwind was going to slow them down, she added, "And we're not supposed to be late!"

Ella Mae allowed herself to drop back as the girls kept pushing on. They were walking backwards facing her now. "See for yourselves, then!" called Ella against the gusting wind. As she spoke she leaned forward, partly to foil the wind and partly to be heard by the two smaller girls. "You can come and stay with us if you can't get home!"

As their companion turned to leave, Rosa and Thelma saw the wind part Ella Mae's straight brown hair cleanly down the back of her head and balloon her dress out in front. It was no use talking to each other. There was too much noise in the air, and the wind would only take their breath away. Instead, they both bent forward and shielded their eyes from flying grit as they continued toward the pick-up point.

The sisters were too busy pushing on through the wind and keeping dust out of their eyes to even look at the breakwater until they were almost upon it.

"Oh dear!"

They both stopped. As wind-driven waves struck the rip-rap, great plumes of spray flew skyward, soaking the path and menacing anything small enough to be sucked into the sea with the returning water.

"What should we do?" Rosa's question reflected the fear they both felt.

As they stood trying to answer this question, the figure of their father appeared at the landing across the water. Waves were crashing ashore there, too. Licks of foam and spray were glancing off the rocks near the landing. The girls watched as their father hauled the row-boat out of its berth and tried to push it into the water. Each time he attempted to launch the craft, the waves washed it back. George finally took off his shirt and waved it at the girls.

With Ella Mae's wisdom behind them, the two sisters did not have to wonder what their father's signal meant. They knew where the older girl lived from walking with her between the post office and her home almost every day. So they turned from the stormy water's edge and headed for Ella Mae's house, where they spent the night. By some miracle that the youngsters never did fathom, George knew to pick them up there the next morning after the sea had calmed. From that day until the following April, Rosa and Thelma's lessons would be studied under their mother's supervision and the bright light of the Aladdin kerosene lamp that hung over the dining room table.

By the time the eldest sisters reached high school age, George and Ruth had discovered the Nova Scotia Correspondence Study Program. From this time forward, the children's winter lessons came from Halifax, were completed and mailed back, then returned to them with grades and comments. Once spring and safe navigation returned, the children would resume their studies at the little green schoolhouse.

Even during the good weather, school for the Millar children was not the same as it was for other children. There wasn't time to join in after-school activities because there was always the long walk to the breakwater. Even if their transportation was not always on time, the children were expected to be. There were no parts for the Millar children in Christmas concerts, nor places in the choir. When concert time rolled around, it would be all but impossible to travel across the bay anyway. Most of the children's play time was at home on the island—among themselves.

> *We were never congratulated or praised for passing provincial exams or getting good marks on our correspondence course assignments. We were expected to do well. That was a given.*
> —*Malcolm Millar*

George and Ruth knew that a life lived on an island was an isolated one. It could not be otherwise. They knew there was no way to keep their children from being outsiders in a community they were a part of only when the water and the weather allowed. For the parents who chose this way of life, the loneliness was a cross worth bearing, but for the children who happened into it, the isolation made an uninvited imprint.

Perhaps the island life was lonely for the Millar children, but it was not idle. There were many chores to be done, and those who were old enough were drafted into service. In the spring, they began with the universally despised task of picking stones from the fields that were later sewn to grain. The children were convinced the stones grew over the winter, since each year there were more to pick from the same patches they had cleared the year before. At haying time the older children would stack the hay in the field, then unload it into the hay mow above the stable. This was distasteful work, too, since it always occurred during the hottest days of summer. Chaff from the freshly cut hay and perspiration from the exertion made an itchy, prickly combination.

In contrast, picking bugs, one by one, from the leaves of young potato plants was an easy job. Each child was given a glass jar containing a small amount of kerosene in which to drop the captured bugs. At day's end, George would count the catch and pay his helpers accordingly. Each hard-shelled adult warranted a five-cent bonus, since adults were hard to find and were responsible for breeding the others. Income from the children's summer work was a supplement to their allowances. In the fall they would use the extra money to increase their personal libraries or buy Christmas presents.

Separation from the mainland aside, there was not much privacy to be had on a tiny island populated by eight people. As Thelma and Rosa approached their teen years, they sought solitude, finding it on large boulders positioned far from each other on the shore, far from the house and far from interfering siblings. These sandstone pieces, sculpted by the sea, had been worn into comfortable seats that would warm in the sun of a fine summer day. Almost daily during the summer, Rosa and Thelma would retire to these peaceful oases to read or enjoy the sight of seabirds flying and diving, waves rolling in to shore, and the occasional fishing boat bobbing on the endless sea.

And what did we do in the long winter evenings? There was no such time. Bedtime came at 7:30 P.M., winter and summer… We were all avid readers—but no reading in bed!
—Rosa (Millar) Mattinson

Perhaps as a way of compensating for their isolation, George fashioned a play area for his children. At the top of a small rise above the house, he cleared some trees, built a picnic table with benches, strung up hammocks made of feed sacks, and hung swings from the remaining trees. After Thelma, Rosa, and Malcolm had left home, George and David built a playhouse. It was named the "Woodpecker Inn" after a bird-shaped handle from a broken milk jug that became part of the welcome sign above the door. Inside were two rooms that housed a stove made from an old five-gallon bucket, a bed, and a wind-up gramophone that had, by now, outlived its usefulness in the house. Here, Minna, David, and Barbara could play with their mainland friends and host sleepovers.

Of course, there were games as well. On winter days, after schooling on the mainland had been given up for the season, the children played Chinese or regular checkers, dominoes, and card games like "Old Maid," "Authors," or "Nations"—but only after their studies were finished. Conventional playing cards were not allowed in the house, though, as a concession to Grandpa Mitchell's belief that they were "tools of the Devil."

There were always books around, too, that the children received as gifts or bought with their allowances and extra money they earned from chores. Besides Mother Goose stories, *Alice in Wonderland,* and *Pollyanna,* each child had a series of books to call his or her own. Included in the library were Nancy Drew, Hardy Boys, Curlytops, Bobbsey Twins, and Dave Dawson books as well as *Anne of Green Gables* and other titles by L. M. Montgomery. Their mother often read them the "Burgess Bedtime Stories" from the newspaper as well.

Despite the isolation, there were two extracurricular groups the Millar children were able to join. One was the Red Cross group, which met during school hours on Friday afternoons and taught children such practical skills as how to properly wash their hands. There was also the Maple Leaf Club, sponsored by the *Family Herald* newspaper, through which children were encouraged to take up pen pals. It was important to Ruth that her children knew how to write proper correspondence, since she wrote often: in letters to her parents in Pugwash, in her journals, and in notes passed along to her friends ashore in Bayfield. Each child was therefore instructed to respond promptly after Christmas and birthdays with thank-you notes to benefactors.

It was through the Maple Leaf Club that something every good Presbyterian knows proved true once again: there are things in even the bleakest life to be thankful for, and there are always people worse off than yourself. It was Ruth who first learned of the Denton–Cox family. They lived on a lightship anchored off the southern shores of England in waters too shallow to navigate but too far offshore to make a lighthouse practical. Without even a scrap of land to walk on, the children likely envied the Millars their farm chores and rock-strewn beaches. The two families settled into a habit of exchanging Christmas and birthday presents that persisted long into adulthood.

Given what it must have been like looking at life from the deck of a ship, being allowed to join in Christmas concert rehearsals was a blessing—even if the Millar children had to miss the actual concert. The lady of the English lightship did not have the church groups that Ruth did, even if Ruth herself was only able to attend meetings in fine weather. Nor would Mr. Denton-Cox be able to get to the mainland as often as George, who could be found daily at Bayfield wharf unloading his lobster catch during the season.

Besides, life on a small island was not all drudgery. Separated from the mainland or not, there were traditions to be kept, and chief among them was Christmas. Official preparations began in November, when George would take advantage of a clear sailing day to make a trip to the post office and return with a sack full of presents. As he withdrew each package from his duffel bag, George would make much of what the presents were shaped like, or sounded like, or who they were from. Then, he would stack them with care on top of the parlour organ where they would stay until Christmas Day. Until that day, the children were not to set foot in the room except to decorate the tree.

November was also when Ruth baked the Christmas cake. Often this happened on November 11, because that was the day George spent in Antigonish marching in the Armistice Day parade. This break in the island routine allowed Ruth to set things right for her project. She began early in the morning by nursing the flame in the kitchen stove. This was a delicate chore with a wood stove and an oven that had no thermometer. The flame had to be just so, and the heat had to feel just right. Years of practice and patience had taught her how round or neatly split the sticks of wood should be, how often to feed the flame, and how to tell by a hand in the oven when there was enough fire.

Meanwhile, her daughters would be cutting up the candied fruit that went into the batter. When Ruth was certain the oven had reached the perfect temperature, and when she could stand her wooden spoon in the middle of the mixing bowl, she poured the batter into a baking pan and slid it into the oven. While it cooked, the children were sent outdoors, or made quiet indoors, lest they disturb the cake's delicate rising. When it had come out of the oven and cooled, Ruth wrapped it up and placed it in the cellar with the other Christmas treats until it was needed.

George would have selected the tree well ahead of time. On summer passes through the Pomquet Island woods, he would have been looking out for and marking the best one. Then, a week or so before the big day, the children would bundle up in their boots, coats, and hats to follow their father into the bush where he would fell the tree and haul it home. This annual event was something George never mentioned to his superiors at the Department of Marine and Fisheries. As described in the government's information for mariners, no tree was to be cut on the twenty-five-acre island in order to preserve its "wooded" appearance. Even the daily firewood had to come from the mainland.

By Christmas Eve, the dining room of the Pomquet Island lighthouse was already converted. Once cold weather arrived, the range was moved from the summer kitchen into this room, where chores could be done in comfort and the stove could help heat the house by way of a stovepipe hole in the ceiling directly above it. Bedtime came promptly at seven-thirty, Christmas Eve or not, so the children hung their stockings from the dining room clock shelf earlier in the evening.

Every year during the Christmas season, the eight-day clock that chimed on the hour, the half-hour, and the quarter-hour was underscored by a jagged row of expectant socks. These were not fancy, once-a-year stockings ordered from a catalogue. These were working socks, the kind the children would pull on before plunging their feet into gum rubber boots and heading for the barn. Each stocking reflected the size and the age of its owner. Mother, father, and baby—and there often was a baby at Christmas—were also represented by some form of knitted footwear.

On Christmas morning—even before George had a chance to extinguish the tower light at dawn—the children clambered downstairs to find each woolen toe stretched bulbous by an orange, a rare and exotic fruit. Every legging was stuffed with Christmas shapes of barley sugar candy in red, green, and gold. This special treat was gathered up and held in trust by their mother, who paid it out gradually over the remainder of the winter. And there was always something special for each child in his or her own stocking. It might be a small pull toy, a tin soldier, a painted doll, or for the baby, a celluloid rattle. These small gifts kept everyone busy until Ruth called them all to the table for breakfast.

When we arrived on the island there was just a small patch of cranberries, but this increased and patches spread all over the island. One fall at least seven bushels of berries were picked, and some were still there to be picked the next spring. The ones picked the next spring never required as much sugar.
—George Millar

In a household where extravagance was sternly frowned upon, Christmas was always a day of plenty. For breakfast, there was potted head that Ruth had carefully seasoned and pressed into its scallop-edged mould a month or so beforehand when George had slaughtered the pig. For the main meal, there was a fully dressed chicken, which had been selected a day or two earlier from the yard. The cranberry sauce came from berries picked on the island. Garden vegetables were brought up from the cellar, along with homemade gingersnaps, mincemeat pie, doughnuts, pudding, and the meticulously crafted fruitcake.

After the first meal of the day, all were permitted to move to the parlour. The room was warm from the fire of the pot-bellied stove that George shook down and stoked with coal when he first came downstairs. The tree stood in a corner of the room, decorated a week or so earlier with pencil twists of coloured paper. No candles would light this tree, though. In a lighthouse where the danger from fire was present enough, no further risks were taken. Under the tree were the gifts that, until the night before, had rested atop the organ. On Christmas Day, they appeared to have been carefully arranged by Santa's own hand.

From Santa, the children received books, although the inscriptions on the inside fly leaves were always in a tightly curled script curiously similar to their mother's. There would be something for the parents under the tree, too. With their money earned picking potato bugs, the children ordered something from the Holman's or Eaton's catalogue. Ruth had devised a system by which each child could indicate on a folded piece of paper the desired gift without her seeing what had been written. The children's order, together with her own gift order, was always packaged off to the post office in time for the Christmas mail. Among gifts from the children might be a Wilf Carter record for George or a pretty pin cushion for Ruth. Grandpa and Grandma Mitchell always sent useful articles of clothing from Pugwash to round things off.

As the years went by, life on Pomquet Island changed. More conveniences, like a wringer washing machine, were added. The younger children were no longer subjected to the same strict discipline that marked the early years of their older siblings, and were allowed to coast down the cliffs and onto the ice of the bay in winter, for example. But the basic limitations remained: there was no electricity, no telephone, and no running water. Thus, the outhouse remained a permanent feature of island life.

As outhouses went, the Pomquet Island one was a cut above many, especially because it was a two-holer. Thanks to George's craftsmanship, one side boasted an adult-sized hole, and the other, a convenient step to a smaller hole for children.

Barbara was about four years old the day she decided to try out the big hole. She, ten-year-old Minna, and eight-year-old David had been amusing themselves on the playground. David was still there, absorbed in some great adventure from which his sisters had now adjourned. It was the older sister's turn to keep an eye on Barbara this summer day, which included accompanying her into the loo.

"That's my side," Minna pointed out to her younger sister as the door swung shut behind them.

Only a tiny, square window placed high on the door and gaps under the eaves of the bare-timbered roof allowed light into the meagre space.

"I want it." Barbara was already at the hole and preparing to lift herself onto the wooden bench, which came just above her waist.

"But you're too small. You need the step." Minna pointed to the hole for tots.

"I want this one!" repeated the younger sister.

The little outhouse, sitting as it did over a pit of accumulated waste, was not a place to linger in any weather. In mid-summer, its users were even less inclined to take their time. It was a warm day, and Minna wasn't about to get into a lengthy debate. "Have it your way, then." She moved to the smaller seat.

As she did so, Barbara hoisted herself onto the adult side by turning her back to the bench, placing her hands on either side of the hole, bending her knees and springing up, backwards. Minna had barely turned her head to her own business when she heard the unmistakable sound of something large falling into the liquid of the latrine. She looked around to find that Barbara had disappeared. An immediate and lusty wail left no doubt as to her whereabouts.

"Let me out! Get me out!" Barbara was screaming the best she could without breathing in any more than she had to.

There was good news and bad news about her fall. The good news was that George had only just cleaned out the pit three months before, as he did every spring. The bad news was that, because the pit had been recently cleaned, Barbara fell farther than she otherwise might have and she was unable to pull herself back up through the opening.

Minna hollered out the door. "Mum! David! Come quick!" Then she sucked in her breath and held it before reaching into the hole to pull her baby sister out. Luckily for Minna, Barbara had landed on her backside so that her hands and arms had not yet been touched by the muck.

"Grab my wrists!"

Minna knew this grip was the one to use when someone fell overboard from a boat, so it would probably work in this case. As Barbara grasped her wrists, Minna gripped Barbara's and pulled. But it was no use. Her younger sister was knee-deep in muck, too far away, and too heavy.

By now, David and his mother had arrived at the outhouse to see what the commotion was about. Barbara was beginning to panic and Minna didn't know what to do.

David ran around to the back of the outhouse and lifted the same hatch he had watched his father prop open to shovel out the muck in the spring. He peered into the space under the two-holer and held his nose. The sight of Barbara standing there, knee-deep in filth, arms high in the air, dress dripping with brown liquid, made David want to sit down and laugh.

"Come up here and pull!"

This cry for help from Minna jolted David into action instead, and he rushed to her side. With each pulling on an arm, they hoisted their sister from the pit and deposited her on the solid floor of the outhouse. Barbara immediately ran outside, bawling at the top of her lungs, covered from ankles to waist in odious filth.

As Barbara exited the building, Ruth hurried toward her, then stopped, one hand to her mouth. It wasn't that she didn't have sympathy for Barbara's plight or concern for her health and safety. It was just that Ruth was wearing a freshly laundered dress and apron, and it was almost time to start cooking dinner. *No sense having the dogs and doing the barking yourself.* Ruth turned to Minna. "You'll have to take her down to the water and rinse her off." After all, Barbara had been Minna's charge this morning. "I'll get the washtub ready and some clean clothes. When she comes back, you can bathe her outside."

My boots were apparently put to sea, as they were beyond saving. I'm sure that, in the process, Minna wished to do the same with me.
—Barbara Millar

And a pitiful sight Barbara was. Her humiliation was complete: David lay laughing in the grass a safe distance away, and her mother had already turned her back and started toward the house. There was nothing Barbara could do but let the tears roll down her cheeks and follow Minna to the shore, with the neat new ankle boots she had gotten for Christmas softly squishing every step of the way.

There is no doubt that Dad's ideas of discipline and obedience came from his military service. When you were told to do something, you did it without question. The way of the transgressor was hard. — Malcolm Millar

George Millar's Law

CHAPTER FIVE

George Millar didn't believe there was a God, he knew it.

This God saw a young and green George through the battle of the Somme on the muddy fields of France, stayed with him as he forced himself "over the top" at Vimy Ridge, and was there for one final, futile push at Passchendaele. The youthful soldier made a bargain back then, when it looked as though the mud, the blood, and war's great roar would never end. Now, delivered whole to a peaceful life and the promise of a family, George was making sure to keep his end of the agreement.

Every morning there was prayer. The children knelt before their chairs and—quiet as mice—contemplated the words their parents read aloud from the Bible. Each day's reading picked up where the previous day's left off, and when the final verse of Revelations had been read, the next day's devotions began with the first verse of Genesis.

Through it all ran the one thread with which George always concluded: "Let us lay aside every weight, and the sin which doth so easily beset us, and let us run with patience the race that is set before us." After these words, the parents would rise. A quick kiss would signal that the prayers were over. It was not a sentimental kiss, nor a lingering one. Perhaps it had on each the bolstering effect of a slap on the back from a comrade-in-arms. Perhaps it signified that, knowing they had God and each other, they were ready to take on whatever might come next. Whatever its meaning, it was with this gesture that the day's work began.

George Millar presided over his children the way an officer might lead his troops: on a no-questions-asked, need-to-know basis. Second-guessing orders was not an option, nor was letting subordinates know the reasons for the orders in the first place. Disobedience was met with the strong arm of the law—George Millar's law. But the punishment was fair—to George's mind anyway—and meted out sparingly. Still, it tended to have a lasting effect.

Malcolm was about ten years old when his father approached him one warm spring evening and set in motion a series of events that culminated in a series of events the son would remember for the rest of his life.

"Take Daisy down to the landing," George ordered, handing Malcolm the black cow's lead rope.

George disappeared without mentioning to Malcolm that he would be bringing around the boat he had anchored some distance up the shore from the landing. His plan was for Daisy to swim behind the boat to the mainland. Once there, George would take the cow to a pre-arranged meeting with a suitor. He would thereby secure a future calf for sale or slaughter and supplement the family's supply of fresh milk in the meantime.

Ignorant of his father's plans, Malcolm began to picture himself as a lone cowboy, like the ones he'd read about. But, as far as he knew, leading cattle by ropes around their horns was not something cowboys did. Herding Daisy would probably be more fitting. He stopped to look around. Sure that he was unobserved, the boy slipped the rope from her horns.

"Get up there, Daisy!" he commanded, swinging the lead like an empty lasso behind her.

But Daisy did not share Malcolm's vision. She might be obliging enough with someone at the front end of a rope, but with that someone now behind her, a whole new world of possibilities opened up. Daisy chose to try the untried and veered off the track. Possibly there was something tasty behind the dense bushes.

"Wait, Daisy! Don't go in there!" Malcolm sprinted on an angle hoping to head her off and steer her back to the track, but he only succeeded in startling the usually placid cow.

"M-m-m-o-o-o-o!"

Daisy charged over the bushes and through the trees. She was completely out of her element now. There was no grass, only sharp twigs and thick branches trying to hold her back. She needed to get out of this trap but didn't know how. She only knew there must be danger because her keeper was running too.

This went on for about ten minutes before Malcolm realized he'd better stop chasing Daisy. Too much jostling was not good for a milk cow. What he needed to do was get her settled down so that he could approach her quietly and slip the rope back over her horns before his father realized what was going on.

"Malcolm!"

Too late. It was George wandering closer from the landing where he'd brought the boat from up the shore. No doubt he'd heard the racket.

"What are you trying to do?" There was exasperation in his tone, and his voice was getting nearer. "Where are you, boy?"

It sounded now like George had reached just about the point where Daisy had broken her new trail into the woods.

"Over here."

Malcolm's voice was small, just loud enough to be heard from the track. He had an idea what was going to happen next. Luckily, Daisy had stopped her rampage. She had stumbled into a boggy spot and stood quietly in a patch of lady's slippers, chewing meditatively on a hunk of weeds she'd picked up along the way. When George finally tracked his son down, Malcolm's excuse that the rope had slipped from Daisy's horns was dismissed, and the rope was applied vigorously to Malcolm's behind.

There were other rules that should have been self-evident, even for a child. It should have been obvious why there was to be no playing on the late-winter ice hills that piled high over the shallows and along Pomquet Island's shoreline, pushed there by the action of the sea and the weight of the ice behind them. Nor should it have been difficult to figure out why there was to be no jumping from pan to floating pan of ice in the spring as the covering on St. George's Bay broke up. Still, children would be children.

> *Had he told me he was taking Daisy to the mainland, I would not have had to sleep on my stomach that night.*
> *—Malcolm Millar*

On a late spring day in 1929, seven-year-old Thelma, five-year-old Rosa, and three-year-old Malcolm were looking for something to do outside when they noticed a couple of ice cakes floating easily in the clear water close to shore. Some time ago, George had appointed his eldest daughter the "Big Boss"—his lieutenant, as it were. So, with Thelma in the lead, the three trooped down a slope and onto the rocky beach to investigate.

St. George's Bay was the picture of calm. There was virtually no wind. Ice stretched all the way from the island's midpoint to the Bayfield shore. It covered the harbour but had by now passed from a solid winter mass to large, floating chunks. It was evident even from shore that most of the floes were rotten, waiting to dissolve into slush and eventually become one with the water. The rest of the bay was a clean, shiny blue, stretching smoothly from the northern tip of Pomquet Island to the hills of Cape Breton in the hazy distance.

But two small pans of ice had broken from the rest of the pack and drifted toward the island, just about in line with a space where the children liked to play. The tide had probably brought them there overnight, and when the water receded they were left behind, too large to float back out through the rocks that studded the shallows. Rosa and Thelma moved in to examine the ice floes more closely. Thelma held up one hand in a stop sign while she inched closer to this new phenomenon.

"Malcolm, you stay there."

The water was only about a foot and a half deep. The surface of the ice sat about four inches above the waterline, with at least that much below. Close up, the apparent white of the ice was grey, and its surface was gravelly with old snow.

They all were wearing rubber boots, because the ground was still too wet to be outside in shoes. Thelma waded into the water, then climbed onto a nearby rock that made a step to the ice floe. Within seconds she was standing triumphantly on the raft of ice and regarding her brother and sister from a frozen stage. She stamped a foot to test the sturdiness of her platform. No movement. She jumped with both feet. Nothing.

"It's safe! Come on!" called Thelma, at the same time moving to the far edge and looking down into the water on the bay side. It was deeper there, but not by much, and there were large rocks not far away that prevented the ice from drifting more than a few yards from shore.

In an instant Rosa was alongside Thelma, and both sisters were reaching out to help their younger brother make the leap from rock to ice surface.

"Wow-ee!"

The children had a whole new view of the world from here. They'd never looked at their island from this angle before, and they'd never viewed the hills across the bay, nor the wharf, from this vantage point. It was almost as if they were sailors on an Arctic sea.

"Let's ice hop!" called Thelma.

The other two followed her to the edge and regarded the foot-wide gap between their ice chunk and the one beside it. Before they knew it, their older sister had cleared the open water easily and was standing on the ice next door, looking back at the lagging troops. Rosa was soon standing beside her sister and they were both regarding Malcolm with some discomfort. He was too small to jump, and his face was just starting to crimp up in what could become a wail if not tended to quickly. So, Rosa and Thelma jumped back again to keep their brother company.

"Malcolm, you watch and see who can jump farther, me or Rosa."

The two sisters were off, jumping back and forth between ice floes, each trying to best the other's distance. The girls' legs were getting heavy and the edges of the floes were wearing down when they began to realize their repeated jumps were forcing the two ice pans farther and farther apart.

"Oh well, it'll soon be time for lunch anyway," reasoned Rosa as the three left the ice behind and trudged toward home.

These children didn't have much practice disobeying their father, but they managed all afternoon to keep news of their Arctic-explorer adventure from leaking to their mother. It wasn't until after supper, when Malcolm was being readied for bed, that the secret was revealed. George, having been on the mainland all day, asked Malcolm an innocent enough question before seeing his son off to bed: "How did you keep yourself busy today?"

Malcolm, being the least schooled in deception, told his father exactly what he had done. "I helped Thelma and Rosa jump on the ice!"

George didn't wait until his anger cooled before he administered the punishment: three short, sharp whacks to the backside with a piece of kindling. Thelma's was the first and most vigorous of all the punishments because she was the oldest and, therefore, was responsible for her siblings.

But he did not stop there. In George's mind, the punishment had to be harsh enough to keep his children off the ice. He had to be sure that even when the memory of the pain had dimmed, the children would not be tempted to take another step onto an errant ice floe. It wasn't enough that only Malcolm's older sisters should get the punishment and that he be let off with a warning. What if Malcolm should see pieces of ice some day and decide to go ice-hopping by himself? No, all three needed to be disciplined.

The lesson was well learned. They never tested the ice again.

The lightkeeping life was one for the practically minded. There was little room for frills, and this was fine with George and Ruth, since they weren't inclined toward frivolous things anyway. Exceptions were articles that, perhaps, could be considered cultural or educational—the organ that Ruth tried to teach her children to play, the battery-powered radio that let in the outside world, the heirloom china, and the gramophone with musical selections that ranged from "Mauri Love Ditty" to "The Capture of Albert Johnston." In fact, Ruth and George took a certain pleasure in using ingenuity to eke out the best that life would allow on the tiny island. For her, it was most likely to come out at the treadle sewing machine, or in her knitting. For him, it would surface in the things that he made in his woodshed workshop.

On an island where self-sufficiency and doing without struck a precarious balance, nothing was ever wasted—not wood, not food, not water, not yarn, not even flour sacks. Even old salt bags became handkerchiefs. Used dishwater went to the pigs along with the table scraps. Cooking fat was saved and later rendered into the raw material for lye soap, which was used to wash those same dishes and—but for laundry—almost anything or anyone else in the house.

Time was not allowed to slip by unnoticed either. Ruth knitted right through the four seasons. There was usually a project sitting on the dining room windowsill waiting for a lull in her other chores so she could add a few stitches. And the project wasn't always for something completely new. Often it was replacement feet for worn-out socks that still had perfectly good legs left in them, or finding a use for leftover lengths of yarn in things like pot holders, squares for lap rugs, or multicoloured mitts for the children. Scraps of fabric remaining from homemade clothes were braided into warm mats for the floor or sewn into quilts. Ruth later made each of her six grown children a quilt in a design she dubbed "Job's Patience." Each quilt was fashioned from scraps of leftover fabric, and of the five hundred squares, no two were of the same material.

In the same spirit, used flour sacks became sustaining pieces in the wardrobe of every female family member. It was a fact commonly known but rarely discussed that there was not a woman in Bayfield who did not owe her steady supply of bloomers and underwaists to one flour mill or another. Ruth would save the coarse cotton bags all winter, then in the summer the laundered material would be laid out to whiten in the sun. Despite the commonness of the practice, it was always best to have "Five Roses Flour" bleached out before the underwear took shape. Maybe the Five Roses people knew this and made their dye weak on purpose. In any event, none of the Millar girls ever had to go to school with red letters stenciled across her backside.

The men typically wore the standard blue Balbriggan knits that came by mail order from Eaton's or Holman's of Charlottetown. Other things came by mail order, too: fabric, for example, that Ruth fashioned into the greater part of the family's wardrobe; the patterns the clothes were made from; leggings for socks so that all Ruth had to knit were the feet; and the yarn to knit the feet, mittens, hats, and scarves. Every spring, Ruth would race to have the children's new fall clothes complete, save for the button holes, by the time her parents arrived on the island to spend their wedding anniversary in June. Then, she would turn the clothing over to her mother, who would finish every hole by hand—not a small job, since bloomers were fastened by buttons to underwaists, and all the outer clothing required buttons, too.

The annual visit by the grandparents was much anticipated by the children, even if Grandpa Mitchell was somewhat of a prude. Despite his dour Presbyterian nature, he always managed to have candy for his grandchildren. Malcolm used to especially look forward to these visits as he approached his teen years, because his grandfather began to trust him with a straight razor. If he didn't draw blood while shaving his elder, Malcolm was awarded twenty-five cents. At Christmas, their grandparents would give each of the children a twenty-five-cent bill called a shinplaster. This was the only paper money the children knew.

One year, when Thelma and Rosa were small and Malcolm was still a baby, Grandma and Grandpa Mitchell gave the family a small table and chairs. The wooden furniture was just the right size for the junior Millars to stage their own meals without straining to fit at the adult dinner table. Not long afterward, a tiny china set was added. When Malcolm grew old enough to sit with his sisters, George began disappearing regularly into his workshop. Eventually, he emerged with a small captain's chair just the right size for Malcolm. The miniature suite logged many years of durable service in a corner of the Pomquet Island dining room.

George built a bobsled early on, too. It held about three people at a time and had four wooden runners, two in the front and two at the back. Both sets were fitted with bands of steel on the bottom to make the sleigh go faster. The runners on the front could be turned left or right for steering.

There were times, rare though they were, when George would ride on this sleigh. When winter conditions were just right, it was safe to slide from the top of the bank near the house all way down to the ice on the bay below. The children were not permitted to try this adventure themselves, but occasionally their father would hop on and steer them on a stomach-lurching ride over the steep bank and far out onto the ice-covered bay. Since not everyone could fit on the sled at the same time, George would take them in turns. But these times were unusual, especially in the early years on the island. Mostly, George was preoccupied with the business of keeping his family fed, clothed, and safe in their voluntary exile.

And there were obligations, not simply to family, but to the church as well. George and Ruth felt these most keenly, but they sometimes struck the children with force, too. Just advancing into their teen years, Thelma and Rosa had no reason to think there was anything unusual about their minister's Saturday night stay on Pomquet Island. It was common for the pastor of the Mulgrave charge—which encompassed Bayfield—to divide his time among the numerous small parishes and billet overnight with families in his congregations.

It wasn't until the boat ride to church the next morning that both teenagers started at Rev. Reynolds's paralyzing intonation: "It's wonderful that you two girls are going to join the church this morning."

George and Ruth flashed wide-eyed looks at each other over the heads of their daughters. It was only then that they recalled their innocent conversation with the preacher the night before, after the children had gone to bed. It came back to them in a flash, then, how they had somehow been convinced that it was time for their two oldest to be joining the church. Come to think of it, they had allowed that tomorrow might be as good a time as any. But hadn't they both believed that, by the time they saw their clergyman into the spare room for the night, they had succeeded in putting him off for a while?

> *If I could have crawled over the side of the boat and swum for home, I would have.*
> *—Rosa (Millar) Mattinson*

But any attempt to ease Rosa and Thelma's palpable anxiety right there in the boat would risk showing disrespect to their clergyman. Explaining to the girls later that their minister had jumped the gun would suggest a disconcerting lapse of command on the parents' part. Even if they hadn't planned the ceremony for today, George and Ruth would put a brave face on it and behave as though this was all part of the master plan. Better too little information than too much—that was George's motto.

It was not so much the thought of committing themselves to the church that made the two sisters' hearts lurch, it was the surprise. Any near-adult satisfaction the teenagers may have taken in being judged fit to undertake this rite of passage evaporated even before it could be formed. The girls would do their best to take the trauma in stride, but the memory would stay with them for the rest of their lives.

If it had ever been put to him, though, George would have acknowledged that his own role model for fatherhood was somewhat skewed. He didn't often speak of it, it but his thoughts must sometimes have shifted back to one lonely day.

It was spring, and raining the kind of cold, steady rain that seems like it won't ever stop, the kind that makes footsteps sink into snow-less grass and leave watery indentations. It was the mud that stuck in George's mind, though. He had just turned twelve, so it must have been late April. His father was climbing back into a borrowed buck-board but George was still standing in Levi Kennedy's barnyard. The area in front of the barn door lay slick with grey mud from the goings in and comings out. In George's memory, he could still see the way Levi's rubber boots slid sideways a bit with the push in each step as he came to meet the wagon.

"Now you listen to Levi, boy, and do what he says." James Millar called this over his shoulder as the horse startled forward and the wagon slid out of the barnyard through the gathering mud and rain.

This was the first young George knew of his family's predicament. His mother, whose mind had not been right since the arrival of his baby sister Annie, had been bundled off to the poor house. His brother William would be sent, like George, to a farm to earn his keep. Sisters Emma and Grace would be placed in similar situations as domestic help. Annie would be taken into the care of his father's sister Mary.

A couple of years later, George met his father in that same barnyard. It wasn't the first time son and father had seen each other since they parted, but their visits had never been long. By now, George's mother had died in that holding pen for people who were too poor or too cra-zy—or both—to look after themselves. George knew of his mother's passing not because his father had told him, but because the Kennedys were helping him keep in touch with his family. He knew, too, that she had been buried in Pugwash under a stone that bore her maiden name, Van Buskirk. George's father had arrived on this day to ask his son to join him on the harvest excursion train to the prairies, where farmers were growing more wheat than they had hands to gather it.

It could not have been easy leaving the Kennedys. They had become almost more like parents than George's own. They allowed him to keep going to school, and even though he was—strictly speaking—the hired help, Mrs. Kennedy would sometimes put a warm hand on George's head or shoulder when he was settled in at the supper table. On the day he left, she couldn't help but let a few tears escape.

"We like you so much we wish we'd never had you!" were her plaintive words as George and his father pulled out of the yard for the last time. Backhanded as the utterance was, George treasured it. The declaration meant he had been valued, loved even. These words became part of family legend as George retold them each time he reminisced about his life with the Kennedys.

George and his father got off the train somewhere around Weyburn, Saskatchewan, but eventually their paths diverged again. Some time later, George had made his way to Winnipeg. By that time talk of the war in Europe was everywhere. Every youngster big enough to shoot a rifle dreamed of signing up and going overseas to fight. These green, would-be warriors had visions of conquering the invaders and sailing back home victorious, all before it was time to harvest the next year's wheat crop. George was one of the lads caught up in the enthusiasm. He signed on with the reserves and told the first major lie of his life: he gave his year of birth as 1896 instead of 1897. This got him into service at age seventeen. On November 25, 1915, at the age of eighteen, George Millar checked in for the real fighting.

Writing down his next of kin on the enlistment papers, George knew only enough of his father's whereabouts to put down Banff, Alberta. He signed his pay, and the balance of his bank account in the event of his death, over to his aunt Mary, who was raising his baby sister Annie back in West New Annan, Nova Scotia. After demobilization in April 1919, George used his army chit for a free train ride to Edmonton, perhaps looking for his father. Even if he did meet up with James in the early days after the war, George would not see his father again until well after George's own growing family was established on Pomquet Island. And James Millar had a good reason for showing up this time: he needed somewhere to die.

James's health had been failing, so he had moved back to West New Annan in 1929 hoping the sea air might improve his condition. In the spring of 1930, he had surgery in Halifax. To hear George tell it, his father had planned to make his future home on Pomquet Island. In reality, James had cancer and only a few months to live.

George's children knew little of the circumstances surrounding their paternal grandfather's arrival on the island. They had barely even made his acquaintance, since he was completely confined to his bed. Now and then, James could be heard calling out for "Mary." No one really knew for sure who he meant—his wife's name was Elizabeth—although he had a sister Mary, the same Aunt Mary who had taken in George's baby sister when the family split up.

The children had seen George building a commode for their grandfather in the woodshed workshop. The sight of their father helping his own father on and off this custom-made toilet was enough to keep them from entering the bedroom, although they had not been told to stay away. In fact, they had not been told anything at all.

Their grandfather's stay came to its inevitable conclusion, but it was in a roundabout way that the children learned of it. Thelma, eight, and Rosa, seven, were returning home after an ordinary school day on the mainland. They arrived as usual at the Suttons's house. This was their final stop each day before walking the last mile or so to the end of the Bayfield breakwater, where their father would meet them with the rowboat. Katie Sutton, who lived with her bachelor brother, David, could always be relied upon for "the daily orders," passed along by George on his regular stop to pick up the newspaper that the two families shared. On this day the spinster, who never referred to George by name, told the two girls "the ugly man" was going to be late with the boat and that they should wait with her until he came.

It was evening by the time their father arrived, and it wasn't until they got to the wharf that the girls realized they would be sharing their boat with a neighbour and a large, wooden box. It was a dark and quiet voyage back to the island with both oarsmen set grimly on their task of rowing this unusual cargo. The box was lashed across the bow behind George and his helper, who pulled an oar apiece. They faced the girls, who were seated demurely in the stern, books on laps, quiet as mice. The oars in the water made the only sound, but tonight there was an added effect. Tiny lights glowed and danced where the paddles parted the water. Mariners knew this rare natural phenomenon as phosphorescence. On this night it was downright eerie.

The next day after school, the girls were again told to wait for their father at the Suttons's place. Katie, seeing their puzzled faces, realized they still had no idea what George was up to.

"The ugly man and Mrs. Millar are gone to New Annan to bury your grandfather," she told them bluntly.

The sisters looked at each other and their eyes widened in unison as they both realized the significance of the box they had sailed with the night before. It was a warm fall day but Rosa shivered. The memory of her grandfather's death would forever be illuminated by the water's ghostly glow.

Like her husband, Ruth was not one to waste time explaining her actions to her children. She was not a demonstrative mother, but she was a loving one just the same. Her love was not a sentimental kind that could always be seen flowing forth. It was a quiet kind, as though she had just placed it there—ready to be picked up when needed, but never forced upon anyone.

This kind of love had worked on George. With years of emotional calluses rubbed hard, he had been a tough nut to crack all right, but nothing Ruth couldn't handle.

It is often said that women marry their fathers, and Ruth's father, David Mitchell, was no teddy bear either. Two of his brothers had given their lives over to the church, so it must have seemed to David that he

LEFT
George Millar before shipping off to Europe in 1915. This was the photo he inscribed to Ruth: "From one who cannot and will not forget you—George Millar."

BELOW
Ruth Elizabeth Mitchell on her twenty-first birthday in 1918, three years before she and George were married. This photo was likely taken at her childhood home in Pugwash. Note the cat— Ruth's home was rarely without at least one.

LEFT
The lighthouse
from the west side,
c.1930.

ABOVE The lighthouse on Pomquet Island, located at the northeastern end of the island, c.1935. The shed to the rear is the oil house, where the kerosene for the light was stored in large barrels. The single-storey wing with the tall flue at left is the summer kitchen, which was added some time after the original building was completed in 1868. The light tower can be seen in the rear of the photo.

A youthful Ruth Millar with (from left)
Rosa, Malcolm and Thelma, c.1928.

Rosa at the front vestibule steps with one
of many cats her mother admitted to the
Millar family over the years. This picture
was probably taken on Rosa's first day of
school in 1928. She is wearing a suit of
red and tan gingham made by her mother.
Thelma, who started school the same day,
had an identical suit. Rosa's hair style
would have been accomplished by George,
who would have placed a bowl on her head
and trimmed around it.

ABOVE Jumbo with (left to right) David, Minna, Malcolm, Rosa, and Thelma, c.1934.

BELOW Minna with the ill-fated Don, c.1936.

ABOVE
David (left) and Minna with
one of the many calves born
on the island, c.1937. Milk
cows were routinely swum
to the mainland, bred and
brought back. This ensured
a supply of milk. The calves
might later be sold or raised
for slaughter.

RIGHT
Malcolm and Barbara
feeding the pig on Pomquet
Island, c.1940. Note that
Barbara has bare feet. The
Millar children spent most
of their summers barefoot
as a way to economize on
footwear.

George and Ruth Millar with the children still living at home in 1940: David, Barbara, Minna, and Malcolm (left to right). Thelma was attending nursing school in New Glasgow and probably took the photo. Rosa was keeping house for her grandparents in Pugwash.

The Millar family, c.1941. Back row (left to right): Rosa, Minna, George, Ruth, Malcolm, Thelma. Front row: David and Barbara.

LEFT

Minna, Barbara, Thelma, and Rosa (left to right) seated on a fish crate aboard a horse-drawn sled, c.1937. The lighthouse is in the background. Note the long woolen leggings and gum rubber ankle boots worn by Minna and Rosa.

BELOW

George and Ruth Millar with their green Volkswagen bus named Samantha, following their retirement, c.1962. The bus made two trips across Canada and several around the Maritimes before it, too, was retired. Lassie did not accompany George and Ruth on their trips, although a pet budgie often did. The identity of the dog pictured here is unknown.

ABOVE An example of a fifth-order 270-degree lens with duplex lamp, much like the one George Millar used on Pomquet Island *(Photo courtesy Barry MacDonald)*.

BELOW Pomquet Island in 2006. The rubble to the left of the new light is the remains of the original foundation. *(Photo courtesy Donald Humphrey—Nature Conservancy of Canada)*.

would have to live a straight-arrow life if he were going to come even close to them in the great weigh-in at the hands of St. Peter.

As a young man, he might have thought losing his first wife through a hole in the ice on a Sunday sleigh ride home from church would be enough, but he knew he must have done something in his second marriage that made God want his first daughter, too. Maybe it was because he'd named her after the wife who'd died. If only he'd been thinking clearly when Martha was born, he would have remembered the old wisdom that said you don't name a baby after someone in your family who has died before their time.

God hadn't been satisfied with even a wife and a daughter. He had taken a son, too. Losing his first-born son had been a terrible blow. But David Mitchell accepted his lessons, thanked God for leaving the remainder of his family, and kept on. He would try his best to teach his surviving children the same outlook.

So Ruth didn't find George Millar's stern nature a bit out of place. Fortunately for her children, she had gravitated more toward her mother's traits. Her quiet love was about her all the time—when she was knitting mittens in a warm corner of the kitchen on a cold Pomquet Island day, or when she was planting pansies in the spring garden to "encourage the vegetables." It made her an oasis of warmth and acceptance on an island of bleakness and solitude. Ruth was the counterbalance to George's aloofness, and he left the nurturing of the children to her. His job was to make sure they were all strong enough to survive in the outside world—and if anyone knew how cruel the world could be, it was George. His attempts at familiarizing his children with this fact sometimes came very early in life, and left lasting impressions.

Malcolm was just a toddler finding his way around the dining room one day while his father sat by the table taking in the previous week's news, as told by the Antigonish *Casket*. The youngster was keen to touch and smell things, to know what they were and how they worked. He tottered toward the opposite end of the table toward a bottle of Minard's Liniment, a sharp-smelling preparation for relieving muscle and joint pain.

With both hands, the young adventurer lifted the bottle from its perch and held it close to his chest. Then he trundled on unsteady legs back to his father's knee, where he deposited the container of liniment, quite content with his conquest. His father, with a look of great benevolence and an air of eager assistance, accepted the bottle, unscrewed the cap, and held it out for his first son to sample. The youngster had barely begun to inhale when the stinging odour of the liniment set him flat on the seat of his rompers on the dining room floor. Malcolm's eyes were red with tears for some time. But the little boy's parents could be quite sure from that day forward that he would never open a medicine bottle unbidden.

And it was also true that George's directness of speech had a way of falling harshly on sensitive ears. This was why Rosa grew up with the certain knowledge that her parents would have preferred her as a boy. Part of the family legend was that George and Ruth's second baby was to have been named Levi. Though George may have seen this story as an expression of feeling for the Kennedys, Rosa saw it as an expression of disappointment that she had been born a girl.

> *Be it known that the Maritime elixir known as Minard's will bring tears to an adult's eye.*
> *—Malcolm Millar*

Ruth could be counted upon to be gentle with her children and, on occasion, to intercede with George—although there was never much direct evidence that this occurred. There was the shoe tack incident, though. It began when George gave eleven-year-old Thelma fifteen cents one morning before school and asked her to run to the general store during lunch to buy tacks that he needed to repair his shoes.

It was the first time George had entrusted her with a job like this, and Thelma felt privileged. Upon completing her purchase, the young shopper was pleasantly surprised to find she had three cents change. What to do? Take it home to her father with the tacks? Or buy some of the maple sugar candy gleaming at her through the glass of the tall bottle on the counter? A reward, perhaps, for a job well done.

"I'll have three cents worth of candy, please." Thelma liked the way she sounded: authoritative, grown-up. As soon as the paper-bagged candy was in her hand, the grown-up-ness was forgotten. Thelma pulled open the store's screen door and streaked through, not waiting to dampen its rattle as it snapped back against the frame. Back at school, she was just in time to hand out candy pieces to her friends before the teacher clanged the bell that called them back inside.

At home that evening, George raised his voice in disbelief. "Do you mean those shoe tacks cost a whole fifteen cents?" He was all but shouting.

Thelma stood in front of her father, hands folded, feet together, head bowed. She couldn't look at him. She could only nod and feel the memory of sweet candy turn sour in her mouth.

"Fifteen cents! Highway robbery! I know Charlie Gass likes to make a dollar, but how can he charge fifteen cents for shoe tacks for glory sake?"

Ruth was busy stirring supper on the stove and George turned to her. "Don't you think that's too much?"

She murmured a noncommittal reply and continued to stir. Then she added, "Come on now, girls, let's set the table."

Glad for her release, Thelma all but ran to the cutlery drawer, then swooped into the dining room and the blessedly clear air.

But George wouldn't let it go. Grudgingly, he recorded the whole fifteen cents in the ledger he kept of each household expense. His disquiet hung over the household the whole evening. All the while Thelma was doing her homework at the dining room table, she could hear him muttering under his breath at intervals, "Fifteen cents for shoe tacks! Highway robbery!"

This was the first crime Thelma had ever committed. Now what was she going to do? How could she have let a moment of weakness take her over like that? What if Daddy went to the store and argued the price? The jig would be up and Thelma would be in for a big one, probably worse than the time she played on the ice. *Be sure your sins will find you out*—these words from scripture kept ringing in her head. Rosa and Malcolm knew what their sister had done—after all, they had shared some of the candy. Did that make them guilty, too? What if they all caught heck for it?

Ruth supervised Thelma and Rosa's prayers as usual that night before they climbed into bed together. "What am I going to do?" whispered Thelma painfully to her sister. "I don't know!" answered Rosa, just as painfully. But Rosa's guilt wasn't as heavy, since she was merely a passive participant in Thelma's indiscretion. Soon the younger sister was breathing evenly, lost in her dreams, but Thelma stayed awake, eyes wide open. *Be sure your sins will find you out.* There was only the moonlight slanting through the dormer window and the whispering of the waves washing the shore for comfort.

The next morning, Thelma heard George tramping down the creaky stairs as usual. Ruth usually stayed in bed for a few minutes, taking in the quiet before the house came alive again for the day. The babies would need to be fed, breakfasts prepared, and children herded off to school. For these few moments, Thelma knew she could catch her mother alone. Carefully she slid out of bed so as not to wake Rosa and crept quietly down the hall to her parents' bedroom. As soon as she caught sight of her mother's face, all caution left her and she dove for the bed, lifting the covers as she went. Snug against her mother's warmth, Thelma confessed to her crime, and sobbed and confessed some more.

Lying with her arm around her oldest baby's shoulder, Ruth said nothing as Thelma sobbed her broken story.

"It was only three cents...and I thought...and...what's Daddy going to do?"

Finally, Ruth peeled her daughter from her chest, wiped her tear-stained cheeks with a corner of the bedsheet and said gently, "You go get ready for school now and we'll not say another word about it."

That was all there was to it. There would be no punishment this time, and no further discipline was required. Miraculously, the boat ride to the breakwater that morning did not include expressions of George's incredulity at the price of shoe tacks, nor was the subject ever raised again.

The whole shore is rock-bound, and there is not a single
foot of space on the whole shoreline not studded with
rocks of varying sizes. —George Millar

But for a Bit of Luck

CHAPTER SIX

Ruth Millar was not the nervous sort so, as the years went by, it ceased to affect her sense of security whether George was on the island or off. She had long since learned to trust her husband's talent for self-preservation and was content to have responsibility for the light station to herself—even during the times George was kept away due to sudden bouts of bad weather or ice. She knew how to operate the lamp if she needed to and, after all, if her own husband couldn't get to her it was unlikely an intruder could. Most visitors to the island arrived by invitation or prior notice. So, when a knock was heard at the door of the Pomquet Island lighthouse, it was an unusual occasion, indeed—doubly so when George was not at home.

The first time it happened was on a foggy day in June. Muffling grey-white mist had moved in quietly one morning and cut the island off from the rest of the world. All the normal harbour sounds of a lobster season in full-tilt had been hushed. When Ruth made her way through this silent shroud to check the tiny shoots of her new garden, the only signal that the rest of creation still existed was the long, low sounding of a foghorn from somewhere across the bay. The seabirds sat still, not speaking. So laden was the air that even childish laughter would fall flat outdoors, if it were heard out there at all. Though the season was verging on summer, it was a good day to stay inside.

George fished lobster to supplement his lightkeeper's salary and, like all of his seafaring associates, had been out tending his traps this day as soon as it was light. He would have been back to the wharf and unloaded the morning's catch before the fog set in. By now, Ruth imagined, he was probably with friends in a fisherman's shack or at the lobster cannery office shooting the breeze, suspended there until the fog lifted. Since Ruth could do no more gardening just yet, she busied herself with the tail end of spring cleaning and some washing up in the summer kitchen. Baby Barbara slept in her basket by the dining room table, and the other children amused themselves by reading or playing the permissible card games.

Then came a rap on the back door. *Knock. Knock.* The sound was so alien to Ruth that she let it go unanswered. *Knock. Knock.* What were the children playing at now? she wondered. *Knock. Knock.*

"Someone wants in, Mumma!" Six-year-old Minna had heard the sound, too, and left her brothers at the table. Ruth noted over Minna's head that Malcolm and David were present and accounted for. Although she couldn't see Thelma and Rosa, she knew they would be elsewhere in the house absorbed in their reading, not roaming outside playing tricks.

"I guess we'd better see who it is." She ran dishwater-damp hands down her apron front and made for the door with Minna close behind.

Standing there, with his back against a grey so thick Ruth could barely make out the trees of the spruce woods behind him, was a man with the unmistakable bearing of a fisherman. He was tall and broad at the shoulders. He wore a wool toque, and the wet of the fog cast it in a misty fuzz around his shoe-leather face. The frayed and sun-bleached shoulders of his long johns dropped from view into chest-high waders held up by a strap over one shoulder. Normally, he'd be wearing a plaid mackinaw shirt, but the day was warm enough to go without.

"Where am I?" The visitor's eyes were wide under middle-aged brows.

"This is the Pomquet Island light."

How could someone stumble across twenty-five acres of rock, dirt, and trees and not know where he was? True, the tower light did not burn during the day—even during this fog—but a man in a boat had to take some responsibility for locating himself.

The man put a hand to his lowered head and scratched at his toque so that it moved side to side and pushed out some stray black hair. Then he turned his face upward, eyes in the direction of the unlit tower and lifted an arm in submission to his would-be guide.

"Aw! Of course i'tis!" He let his hand drop back to his side. "I shoulda known that! Fog's got me all turned around!" He reached up again and peeled off his hat. "I'm sorry ta disturb ya, ma'am."

Ruth nodded. "Where are you coming from?"

"Aw, jest up shore." He made a vague gesture toward the northwest, then used both hands to plaster the toque back on.

"Got a load a lobster fer Irving's."

He was referring to the lobster cannery at Bayfield wharf that was owned by H. Fred Irving. Ruth guessed he must have been coming from somewhere farther along the western shore of St. George's Bay. Perhaps he had blundered into the fog just as he'd blundered into the island, or perhaps he set sail before it settled in. At any rate, he must not have reckoned on how bad the travelling would be in a fog this heavy. Whatever the answer, he wasn't saying now.

"Where's the wharf?"

Ruth stepped onto the damp grass, with Minna close behind clinging to her skirt. Her motion caused the caller to back away and make room. She faced almost due south and pointed.

"It's that way."

But neither could distinguish clear forms of any kind beyond the end of her finger.

To the south of the buildings is a large group of scattered rocks of various sizes, the largest being over six feet in height, only covered at very high tide. These rocks are named the Seal Rocks, for during the late summer and early fall they are literally covered with seals. During the night on the island, one might waken and hear the seals moaning and groaning in chorus.
—George Millar

"It's about a mile from here. You'll have to move well out to the east, though, to get around the sandbar. If you go straight from here, you'll run into it."

"I know where I am now. I'll be all right. Boat's just down there."

He pointed in the general direction of the bank near the house. Miraculously, he had already missed running aground on the Seal Rocks, which jutted out at the island's northeastern tip, just off the lighthouse. If he could do that, maybe he could also avoid a half-mile long sandbar that snapped out like a kite's tail off the shore to the southeast.

Ruth turned to look at her guest. Large as he was, he seemed an amiable enough chap.

"Why don't you come in for some tea and wait for the fog to lift?"

"Naw. Thanks anyway, ma'am. I better keep goin' while m'lobster's fresh."

He turned with a half nod toward her and lumbered off, black waders making rubbery sounds as he went. Ruth could see he was following a track he'd made in the misted grass from the general direction of the Seal Rocks. Soon afterwards, she could hear the distant yet unmistakable sound of a one-lunger marine engine sputtering to life and fading off into the distance. There was no news that day or the next of a fisherman being lost, so she had to assume the sheepish stranger had made port safely.

Later that year, on a warm August night as George relaxed in the kitchen with the newspaper after a long day, there came another knock at the door. When George answered it, he was met with the familiar question: "Where am I?"

This time, though, the air was perfectly clear, but the confused sailor hadn't been aware of the Pomquet Island light. He told George it put him off as he attempted to deliver his passengers at Harvre Boucher some twenty miles to the southeast, near the Strait of Canso. It was George's turn to point the confused mariner in the right direction.

But the wayward sailors who took the cake for the most off-course were the two who surprised themselves with a late-December visit to Pomquet Island.

At six o'clock one evening during the week before Christmas, it was already well after dark and there was a light snow falling. St. George's Bay was still free of ice, and the Pomquet Island light would continue burning nightly until mid-January. It was milking time and George was stepping out the back door, lantern in hand, when he heard the familiar sound of a one-lunger engine. To George's ear, long accustomed to the comings and goings in Bayfield Harbour, it was obvious the unseen craft was too close to the shoal. If it did not change course, it would run aground on the rocky ledge that skimmed under the surface, just off the Seal Rocks. All the locals knew the shoal was there, so this boat must be strange to the area.

At a point near there (Harvre Boucher), the highway used to come over a hill, and with traffic quite heavy at that season of the year, the car lights made a very good guide. So, with the assistance of a compass and the approximate course (which I provided), the man and his party had no trouble making port by using the two guides.
—George Millar

George ran to the edge of the bank and waved the lantern as a signal to keep off. Instead of changing course, the sailors cut their engine and called out from the darkness, "Where are we?"

George's swift reply did not seem to register with the boaters, who were closer to the island than even he had guessed.

The scrape of wood against stone that told George his fear had come to pass. As he scurried down to the beach with a long pole he'd hastily grabbed from the woodpile, he could just make out the forms of two men on the deck of a large fishing boat. Thankfully, the wind was still blowing only lightly from the east and there was no ground swell to dash the boat against the rocks. But George knew the smell of a nor'easter, and he could smell one now. He only hoped the two men would keep their wits about them while he helped extricate their troubled craft and point them to safety. As it was, George could see their judgment was clouded—one man jumped overboard and began trying to swing the boat's bow out.

The day had been one of those that, to the nautically minded, forebode no good. Most of the day it had been snowing lightly with an eerie stillness in the air. Then came a gradually increasing east wind. This told us who have observed his moods over a period of years that old Thor was about to break loose from his stronghold in the north, ready to wage war on all in his pathway.
—George Millar

George quickly waded into the water and passed his makeshift staff to the other crew member. With one of the men in the bow using the pole and the two in the water at the stern, they wrestled the boat free. But George knew this was only half the battle.

Still, he was determined to take their plight one step at a time. The next order of business was to help them safely to the Pomquet Island landing on the lee side of the island. There they could anchor the boat in a sheltered spot before walking to the house for some dry clothes and a hot meal. So George took his lantern back to shore while the two visitors started up their boat. He used this light to guide them northward, past the lighthouse, around to the western side of the island and all the way to the landing.

Once they got to the house, Ruth made the men a hurried meal and found an old pair of George's pants to give to the wet stranger, but there was little time for chit-chat. There was no way the men could spend the night because there was nowhere for them to keep their boat away from the weather, which was just now promising to whip up a good storm. A small kedge anchor was keeping the vessel in place just offshore, but it would be no match for the swell from the blow George knew was coming.

The two men had been fishing cod off the northwest coast of Cape Breton near Chimney Corner during the late fall. Because the day had dawned calm, they decided to head for home at Philips Harbour in Chedabucto Bay, on the south coast of mainland Nova Scotia. As a light snow started to fall, they began to lose their bearings. While following along the shoreline of St. George's Bay, they missed the entrance to the Strait of Canso, which would have taken them straight toward their home port. Instead, they had continued along the south coast of the bay toward Bayfield and Pomquet Island. When they picked up the Pomquet Island light, they thought they were looking at the light on Bear Island in the Strait of Canso.

Occasionally, when the snow would let up, the men caught glimpses of the Cape George light, which was to the north of Pomquet Island. To their disoriented minds, they were seeing the Sand Point light at the south entrance of Canso Strait. In other words, they were heading in exactly the opposite direction. Once outside of Cape George, the two mariners would have been heading for the Gulf of St. Lawrence and into the yawning mouth of a winter gale. When George first told them of their actual location, the men were completely bewildered at how they had managed to travel so far in the wrong direction.

They would now have to sail to Bayfield wharf, tie up, and wait out the storm in a fishermen's hut. George just happened to have a key to one, so he gave it to his guests, along with specific instructions about how to get there and what to do when they arrived.

The storm moved in later that night and raged for two days. The worst of winter had settled in over St. George's Bay. Eventually the two travellers, weary of waiting for good weather fit to sail home to Phillips Harbour, had their boat hauled onto shore where it remained until spring. But their bad luck did not end there. They returned in finer weather to bring their boat home, and while they were inspecting the inside of the tarred hull, a cigarette butt or discarded match touched off a fire. With the help of locals, some sand, and wet seaweed, the fire was brought under control. Humbled by their experiences, they put their boat in the water and sailed for home, never to be seen near Bayfield again.

> *Remembering how we awoke in the morning hearing the wind and snow whistling around the lighthouse, I shudder to think of what might have happened to those chaps, but for a bit of luck.*
> *—George Millar*

The lightkeepers on Pomquet Island did not reserve all of their concern for humans gone off-course. The island had its share of four-legged visitors, too. It was typical in the spring for deer to swim over to the island and spend a few days with the Millars. One year, two swam over to the island, and three swam back.

Animals were not always able to make the entire crossing, however. One fine Sunday the family was rowing to the mainland for church when they spied a dark patch in the water that appeared to be moving. As they neared, they realized it was a waterlogged sheep trying ever-so-hard to keep its nose above water, thrashing steadily farther from land. George manoeuvred the boat alongside while Ruth and Rosa reached overboard and grabbed handfuls of wool to hold the sheep afloat and tow it to shore. There they left the animal shaking, exhausted, and barely able to stand, while they continued to their destination. When the family returned to the breakwater after church, the sheep was nowhere to be found.

The question of how a lone sheep came to be swimming in Bayfield Harbour on a fine Sunday morning remained unanswered until George saw a dog chasing sheep near the breakwater one day. This, he surmised, was what had happened to the waterlogged sheep—it had taken to the water while being pursued by the dog.

Most of the Pomquet Island cattle and horses knew how to swim. That was usually how they got there in the first place. But some took to the water more eagerly than others. One morning, as George strolled to the barn to milk the cows, he noticed that one was missing. The whole family searched the island high and low, only to come to the conclusion that the cow was not on the island, so they continued their search ashore. Sure enough, there was the cow in the first barn they came to, wearing a bell and contentedly chewing her cud. Evidently, this cow had no fear of the quarter-mile swim.

At the other end of the spectrum was the horse, Prince, who never did get used to the sight of breaking surf, despite having swum to and from the island a number of times during his lifetime. On his maiden voyage to the island, Prince made a run for it after being led into the water. As he fled, he towed the boat all the way back to shore, then ran for cover. George and David later found the horse in the same barn the wayward cow had briefly called home.

But Prince the horse also developed a fear of Lucy the pig who, in turn, had a fear of the wind. Whenever there was a strong breeze, she would wail in a voice that sounded something like a cross between bagpipes and a rusty hinge. This became a problem, since there was almost always a wind blowing across the island. And if Lucy's song was annoying to the human inhabitants, it was downright frightening to Prince, who would balk every time he was asked to pass Lucy's pen. This was a problem, too, since the pigpen was near the most-travelled area of the barnyard. Nevertheless, David, in particular, enjoyed the challenge of the horse's balking and rearing when faced with either sow or surf. He would climb aboard the unwilling animal and, from this position,

If you were riding the horse by the pigpen, he would rear and pitch to try and keep from going by. To me this was great sport, as I considered myself to be quite a horseman.
—David Millar

usually convince the horse to do what he was asked to do—albeit after some delay.

Perhaps appropriately, Prince died in old age from an apparent heart attack while swimming to the mainland behind George and Ruth in the rowboat. Ruth had been holding the end of his lead line, and George could hear her remarking to her charge, "If you would keep your head out of the water, you would do better."

Only then did they realize Prince was in mortal distress. Vulnerable to upset in an open rowboat, and as far from dry land as they were, George and Ruth could do nothing to help their struggling companion. There was just time to slip Prince's halter off and row clear before he sank beneath the waves.

Aside from the mythical stork who brought Malcolm, and the seagulls who seemed to enjoy the tease of diving at, but always missing, the tops of people's heads, there was another unpredictable overhead visitor. As the only structures of any height on an otherwise flat island, lightning was often attracted to the buildings on Pomquet Island.

Such a blast of sulphur and brimstone fumes assailed our nostrils that we looked about for his satanic majesty in some corner of the room!
—George Millar

One summer afternoon, while George was entertaining the minister in the parlour, a storm developed. It wasn't often George had someone all to himself with whom he could discuss the gamut of world issues that he read about in the newspapers and heard about on his battery-powered radio. By the same token, Rev. Reynolds, from St. Matthew's in Afton, needed only a little encouragement to hold forth on just about any topic. So the two men paid little heed to the rumblings and flashings outside the windows. Suddenly there was a flash so bright and a crash so loud that George and the minister broke off their conversation and rushed to the dining room.

They arrived just in time to see smoke rising from behind the radio.

Luckily, there were no flames, but when the haze cleared, both men were shocked by what they saw: a black patch the size of George's two hands on the wall behind the radio and scorch marks on the window curtain next to it.

At the same time, Malcolm entered the house looking rather pale. He had been walking from the woodshed to the house when a sudden clap and sizzle filled the air around him with flying splinters. Only after he'd squeezed inside the back door, hands covering his head, was he able to register that lightning had struck the pole that supported the radio antenna on the woodshed roof.

From inside, George and the minister saw the result of the lightning charge, which had evidently traveled along the antenna wire from the shed to the radio in the dining room. When Minna and David emerged from the cellar where they had been playing, they reported seeing a ball of light following a ground wire and disappearing into the clay floor.

Perhaps it was the presence of the clergyman, or perhaps it was just plain luck, but the damage was confined to the radio's speaker and its lightning arrestor—which George declared had, in fact, "resisted arrest." Whatever the reason, the Millars were fortunate to have escaped the strike relatively unscathed—many other lightkeepers had not been so lucky.

Entertaining the minister occasionally was one of the ways the Millars kept up their connection with St. Matthew's United Church in Afton. It was less than five miles away, but it might as well have been five hundred miles in the winter. Even on a fine day in the summer, it took more than an hour to get there, first by boat to the breakwater, then by family car that George kept in a shed at the wharf. Still, the Millars attended services almost every Sunday in the warm months, wind and weather permitting. These days were social occasions, too: sometimes, fellow churchgoers on the mainland would ask them to stay for dinner.

Many Sunday afternoons were spent with the Hulberts, who lived on the farm across the road from St. Matthew's United. Lena Hulbert was a long-time friend of Ruth's, even if the friendship was kept up mostly via notes and exchanges of reading material passed on through George when he made his routine trips to the mainland. For many years, Lena, her husband Edward, and their son shared the place with Edward's father. Eventually Edward died of tuberculosis, which he had contracted while overseas during World War I. After his death, Lena and their son spent a few years on Pomquet Island helping with the housework after Minna, the fourth of George and Ruth's children, was born. Once Thelma and Rosa were old enough to help with the small children, Lena moved back to the mainland.

As a way of returning this hospitality, and as a way of compensating for church services missed during the winter, Pomquet Island, with its great vistas over St. George's Bay and its misty outlook toward the purpled coastline of Cape Breton, was a frequent location for church picnics. George used his motorboat to ferry over the guests, each with a contribution to the picnic in hand.

We often speculated on the outcome of that hug had it been delivered!
—George Millar

One such day dawned warm and sunny with high clouds and a light breeze from the west, holding the promise of perfect picnic weather. But just as George was making the crossing with the last boatload of guests, a sudden rain shower struck. The passengers soon discovered that few experiences could be wetter than travelling in an open boat on the water during a downpour. By the time the small group landed, they were soaked, even though the rain shower was now gone and the sun was shining as brightly as ever. Ruth set about finding clothes for the women to wear while theirs dried on the clothesline.

But George was in the mood for mischief. Dripping from head to toe, he spotted his wife's yellow and black plaid dress, and thought it would be a good idea to give Ruth a damp bear hug. George realized at the last moment that it was not his wife at all, but one of the women who had been caught in the downpour a few minutes earlier.

Ruth did not travel to the mainland as frequently as George, but it was not because she was not able. She simply did not have the time. Early on in their lighthouse life, George had taught her how to row a boat. It was something she may not often have to do, they reasoned, but something she would need to know. By the time Thelma and Rosa had reached school age, she was well practised, having found her skill useful on more than one occasion when George was not readily available. But, as is usual when something is well rehearsed, the performance looks easier than it actually is—especially to the unschooled eye.

One early June day, George and his sometime-hired hand, Everett Guerro, were unloading a few lobster traps onto the shore near the lighthouse to make quick repairs. The lobster season was short, and every broken trap—even for a day—meant a lost opportunity. Everett was sliding one along the gunwale of the small tender they used to ferry themselves between the shore and the lobster boat, which was anchored farther out in deeper water. George, standing on the shore, would take each wooden trap from his helper and place it on the rocky beach.

Everett saw Ruth first. "Afternoon Missus Millar."

Ruth was always charmed by the broad smile that lit Everett's dark face every time he addressed her. He glanced up at the seagulls hovering overhead, bright white against a plain blue sky. They were looking for leftovers still caught in the traps, but there were none. The two men had already picked them clean and landed their catch at the wharf.

"Great day!" Everett added with a nod, then nodded again toward Ruth's friend Mary just a couple of steps behind her. "Afternoon, ma'am."

Mary was visiting from Pugwash and had never seen a black man until she was introduced to Everett a couple of days previously. She still didn't quite know how to behave around him, so she smiled wanly and mumbled a greeting. It was rare for Mary to be at a loss for words, and her presence on Pomquet Island was a change. It wasn't that George and Ruth never talked, but they usually only spoke when they felt they had something worthwhile to say. Mary was different—she liked to fill the silent spaces whenever she could.

In many ways, Mary seemed to be Ruth's opposite: she was of a darker complexion and had a more strident voice, which she used often. Mary was large, what people might refer to as "big-boned," yet she was slim enough to be thought of as wiry. Even her blunt-cut brown hair had a kind of assertiveness to it. Despite their dissimilarities, the women had grown up together in Pugwash, and years of common experience had made them good friends. Mary's presence on the island made it a full house. There were now four Millar children, so mary would stay in the downstairs guest room, while Everett—who made the journey from Guysborough County every spring—was temporarily lodged in a curtained-off section of the upstairs hallway. George and Ruth had one bedroom upstairs, Thelma, Rosa, and Malcolm had another, and the third was occupied by Lena Hulbert and her yound son. The Hulberts had arrived the previous winter to help with household chores. Lena was there now with Malcolm and Minna, allowing Ruth a chance to entertain her guest.

Ruth turned to George, who still had his back to her while he grappled with a waterlogged trap. "It's going on four o'clock," she reminded him.

Thelma and Rosa, aged nine and seven, would be waiting at the breakwater promptly at four o'clock according to their father's own standing orders. He turned to regard his wife.

Sometimes our mother brought us home from school because Dad fished lobsters and couldn't be available to do the ferry work. When he did get us in the afternoon, it was in the lobster boat. Usually it was later than four o'clock when he arrived at the wharf, but the four o'clock rule held for us.
—Thelma (Millar) Beairsto

She was standing with one hand shading her eyes, the other resting loosely on one hip. The sun brought out the shine in her hair, and she was wearing one of George's favourite summer dresses. It had pink and blue flowers against a white background. That print always picked up the colour in her face.

George still didn't say anything, but glanced toward the two remaining traps in the boat. There were a couple of torn heads and some slats that needed replacing. He didn't need to speak to show he was reluctant to leave. Even Mary could see that.

"Why don't Ruth and I pick up the little ones?" she offered, wanting to be useful.

"I guess we could." Ruth looked toward the house. She didn't like to leave Lena too long on her own.

"It's a beautiful day for a boat ride." Mary was becoming convinced a trip to the mainland was the right thing. "Let's go, Ruth. It'll be fun!"

Ruth turned again to her husband. He nodded in Mary's direction. "It'll be a good change for you." Then he strode off after his damaged traps.

So it was Ruth and Mary who met the two oldest girls at the break-water that day. It happened that the children had picked up a letter from Pugwash on their way by the post office. Thelma reached into her school bag for the envelope and handed it over to Ruth.

"Oh! It's from your Aunt Annie. About time! Haven't heard from her since Christmas."

Ruth folded the envelope and slipped it into a side pocket of her dress. She always sewed pockets into the dresses she made, and this very action confirmed the practicality of them. She patted the pocket flat to be sure the letter would not drop out.

Mary knew Annie, too, and she could tell her friend was eager to read the letter from George's youngest sister. Here was another way Mary thought she could be useful. She had seen her small hostess pulling on the oars and moving the boat across the mirror-smooth water from the island. How difficult could that be?

"You go ahead and read the letter, Ruth. I'll row us back."

Ruth started to agree, then paused. "Have you rowed a boat before?"

She didn't recall having seen Mary row a boat when they were children in Pugwash. Now she lived inland and her husband, like her father, was a farmer.

"No, but it can't be that hard. Let me try."

Ruth made sure the boat was safely away from the breakwater, then relinquished the sweeps to her friend and opened the envelope. It was a long letter that covered both sides of two pages in Annie's neatly compact handwriting. To save using only part of a third sheet, Annie had compressed all she could sideways into the margins of the two pages she had already filled. It took some effort to follow the cramped script, but Ruth was accustomed to this type of economy. She had transported herself well into the ink, deciphering the latest news about Annie, husband Aubrey, the three children, and the two new sows, when a splash and a thump against the bottom of the boat made her look up. Ruth was staring directly at the soles of Mary's shoes.

Rosa and Thelma knew they should never laugh at an adult, but they couldn't help it. They had seen the whole thing: Mary's first few strokes with the oars had been tentative enough but then she'd found her stride and had taken to it with gusto. Mary had taken one long, hard pull on the oars with such force that she'd lost her balance and fell over backwards. When the commotion died down and Mary had righted herself, the true impact of her enthusiasm became apparent. The oars were slowly drifting away from the boat, already out of arm's reach.

"Oh dear! What have I done?" Mary's determination to help had set them all adrift, and the import of her blunder was sinking in. "Oh my goodness, Ruth! What will we do now?"

Ruth knew that Mary's reactions could sometimes be over-the-top. So, the hostess did not trouble to get ruffled over something she knew could be easily rectified. There would be another set of oars in the bottom of the boat. Thus, Ruth took her time folding Annie's letter and putting it away in her pocket. "Don't worry, Mary. There's another..."

Now Ruth recognized a predicament. She and Mary were both staring at the bare hull of their boat. There were no spare oars.

"Lord help us!" Mary's hands flew to her face. She was starting to panic, looking left and right. "We're adrift!"

Before another word could be said, Mary was leaning over the side and paddling with her hands. Rosa and Thelma followed her lead. But from her view at the stern, Ruth could see that method wasn't going to get them very far. Meanwhile, the oars rested lazily on the glassy surface of the bay, moving slowly but steadily away. At least both were headed in the same direction.

The boat and crew were about halfway between the breakwater and the island. The question for Ruth was whether to go after the oars first or to land her passengers and then try to catch up with the oars before they made their way out to sea, drifting farther apart as they went.

Rosa stopped paddling momentarily and turned a water-splashed face to her mother. "We could swim after them!"

Ruth knew that was a bad idea. "No we can't. It's too deep and they're too far away."

There must be something in this blessed boat that could be used to row with. Ruth turned around and opened a hatch at the stern. Inside were some lengths of rope, an old buoy, and a large, empty can that was to be used for bailing in the event of leaks or waves over the side. Ruth took the can to the centre seat, leaned over the side, and began pulling it through the water. This might work; the boat was moving. Using the open end of the can as her oar, Ruth brought the boat to shore by scooping through the water on alternating sides.

Rosa and Thelma knew what was coming as they approached the Pomquet Island landing, so they were already removing their shoes and socks. As soon as Mary realized what they were doing, she followed suit. When the water was shallow enough, the three jumped out of the boat and did their best to tow it onto the beach. They couldn't get it up as far as George could, though, so Ruth had to take her shoes off, too.

Once ashore, Ruth handed the boat's mooring rope to Rosa. "Hold this." Then, to Thelma: "Come over here and help me find an oar."

The two girls, along with a still contrite and muttering Mary, scoured the landing for implements, but the only thing they could find was the blade end of one broken oar. Ruth was in too much of a hurry to wait for something better, so she left the remainder of her crew on the shore, hoisted herself back into the boat, and made for deeper water using a blade that was just slightly more useful than the bailing can she'd landed with.

Mary, standing out like a flagpole above Rosa and Thelma on the beach, called after Ruth: "I'll tell George what's happened!"

It was about the only useful thing she could do.

Ruth was becoming adept at leaning over the side of the boat, sinking a makeshift paddle into the water, and bringing the boat forward. Twice on one side, twice on the other, and so on. Soon, she could make out the forms of the two oars, still floating serenely and still heading out into the bay. By now, Ruth was sweating, her hair was beginning to loosen from its pins, and her dress was smudged from close contact with the boat. But the gap was closing on the wayward oars. A few minutes later she had one in her hand. At last she could sit up straight in the seat and paddle—a relief to her aching back. Reaching the other oar would be easy.

Ruth looked around her now for the first time since she'd picked up the foremost oar, and what she saw gave her a fright. Bearing down on her from some distance away was a good-sized lobster boat. It was one of the new Cape Islanders, larger and more powerful than its predecessors, built to run on a car engine rather than the traditional one-lunger. Immediately, Ruth realized she'd groped her way out into the channel that served as the highway to and from the fishing grounds farther out in the bay. She'd never been this far from shore before. Pomquet Island seemed disconcertingly small in the distance.

It would be obvious to anyone that there was a story behind the sight of a housewife in a flower-print dress, sitting in a rowboat in the middle of the channel. That story—or what the story was imagined to be—would likely amuse the men back at the wharf for a few days to come. There was no time to think about that now, though. The other oar was still riding the current out to sea. Ruth kept on paddling and closed the gap. Within a few minutes, she had the second oar in hand.

But the space between Ruth's rowboat and the much larger one motoring steadily toward her was also closing. A familiar bright blue hull with "Annabelle" stenciled high on the bow was pressing toward her. Ruth heard the engine cut to an idle and the swish of water as it parted under a wooden keel. She braced herself for embarrassment. Harvey Gillis could have easily given Ruth a wide berth, but he deliberately came close so that he could get a clear view. Ruth could see the fisherman's mate push up halfway from his seat on the opposite washboard and stretch his neck her way for a good look. Harvey was standing in the open cabin with one hand on a cast-off car steering wheel. As he came within earshot, he doffed his cap and called.

"Afternoon, Missus Millar!"

The larger vessel was slipping easily by and leaving plenty of room, but it was causing enough of a ripple to make Ruth's craft pitch slightly from side to side. From his elevated position, Harvey lowered a shoulder towards Ruth and peered downward into the lurching boat. He could see her fighting against the swell to put the oars safely back into the oar locks.

"Yer good there are ya, Missus?"

Ruth was thinking how good it would have been to see him about an hour ago, but she nodded. "Yes, thank you, Harvey. I'm fine."

As if to demonstrate, she rested her hands on the now-secure oars and gave her fingers a bit of a flutter.

Harvey turned his face toward the wharf and increased his throttle, smiling broadly all the while. He called parting words over his shoulder, and Ruth could hear the laughter in them. "A great day to be out on the water!"

Ruth knew that wouldn't be the slant he'd put to it when he got to the wharf, but she waved and smiled anyway as the *Annabelle* left her behind. "Indeed it is."

She dipped her blades into the water and started for home.

*There have been sunny days and dull ones, calm seas
and troubled sailings. But thanks to the guiding of the
Master Pilot, we always made the harbour safely.*
—George Millar

Thanks to the Master Pilot

CHAPTER SEVEN

George was getting antsy. Ruth could see it, although she kept her thoughts to herself. The evidence was in the small, strange things she would catch her husband doing, like putting on his boots and jacket and walking back and forth from the house to the landing two or three times a day for no good reason, or climbing the light tower with no obvious purpose other than to stare, lingeringly, out over the partly frozen harbour. It had been eight days since he'd been ashore, and George was feeling like a sailor too long at sea.

"You're not likely to make it freeze up by looking at it," was Ruth's dry greeting as George shuffled into the dining room from the stairs he'd descended for the second time that morning. George's answer was a windy grunt as he settled into his rocker by the stove. Even family starts to get to you after you've been cooped up for so long. Ruth understood this, although she had long ago become used to being captive here. Right now she was telegraphing disinterest in her husband's predicament by keeping her own eyes on the bread dough she was mixing up at the dry sink next to the table.

With the arrival of winter and the closing up of the summer kitchen, this room became the general gathering place where most of the household business was transacted. George lifted the teapot from where it had been steeping since breakfast at the back of the stove and poured himself a cup.

"I think I'll try again after this. Looks like the gap might have closed up overnight."

Ruth could smell the tea from where she stood. It was much too strong for her by now, so she kept on with her chore and didn't look up. "Don't come back wet."

"We're not supposed to play on the ice." It was something seven-year-old Minna had been told often enough, and she said it almost under her breath and without thinking, engrossed as she was in the game of dominoes now under way at the dining room table. George glanced at his children over the rim of his teacup but said nothing.

He wouldn't be playing on the ice. If asked, though, he might be hard-pressed to draw the distinction between him picking his way, one step at a time, over barely-safe ice and his children hopping from one wobbling ice pan to another. But when you knew every dip and rise in the bottom of the bay between the island and the mainland as well as you knew each puddle and bump on the track between your house and the landing, when you'd seen ice in all shapes, thicknesses, and conditions come and go for more than a decade, you lost your fear of it enough to study it—enough to get a feel for the enemy.

And poor ice was an enemy. Of all the forces of nature working against civilized life on a small island, this one proved the most formidable. Even in the coldest of winter chills, the harbour's cover could never be counted upon to remain solid from one day to the next. Wind and the pressure of miles of sea ice pushing toward shore could open up cracks, even in cover that was more than a foot thick. As fall or spring moved along, the ice might form a solid sheet, but be unsafe to support any amount of weight. At other times, mild weather might start a break-up, not leaving enough open water to row a boat, but not leaving enough unbroken ice to walk across either.

Still, the enemy hadn't reckoned on George Millar. For seven days he'd tried, and for seven days George had been forced to turn back only a few hundred yards into a crossing to the mainland because the ice cover was just not safe. All week, it had been blowing back and forth, solid one moment then broken up an hour later. Today, George had been watching since early morning, and nothing had changed in the variegated white and black of old and new ice that now covered the harbour. Perhaps today would be the day. After two straight nights of real cold, and with this the second day of calm, it looked as though the crossing might be safe. He'd finish his tea, then set out for the landing. With any luck he'd be back in time for dinner at noon.

Going to the mainland almost every day, either by boat or on foot, was a major feature of George's lightkeeping routine and helped him manage the voluntary exile. He would never admit it, but he treasured the camaraderie with his mainland cronies—especially in the winter when there were fewer to be found. There wasn't much reason for a fisherman to chill himself at the wharf in the cold months

The first winter we were on the island we could drive with the horse or go in a boat, just as we wished. These conditions existed for over a week, but the wind and swell spoiled our bridge in a few hours. There seemed to be no set pattern as to how long we would have an ice bridge— or if we would have one at all.
—George Millar

but there was always someone hanging around at the store, or checking in at the post office, which was where George was headed.

He had been waiting to hear from his superiors at the Department of Marine and Fisheries about the cistern he'd requested so he could collect washing water in the cellar. As well, there would probably be letters from Ruth's family in Pugwash. There might even be something from his sisters in Manitoba. They usually wrote at this time of year, when they had more time away from the farm chores. There was also the newspaper from Halifax to keep him up with the news. Of course, George had the battery-powered radio at home, but its use was carefully rationed. Besides, there was nothing like a good set-down with the paper and a cup of tea in the morning. He'd read the last newspaper front to back so many times that Ruth warned him against wearing holes in it.

George drained the last of his tea and stood. On his way to pick up his jacket and put on his boots, he set the empty cup in the dishpan waiting in the summer kitchen sink. Thelma and Rosa had already washed the breakfast dishes, so his cup would be starting a fresh load. As he passed through the back porch, George grabbed his most important tool for crossing on the ice. It was a stout pole about six feet long that he had fashioned early in his life on the island. He used it to test the ice as he walked, and always held it ready to throw across a hole and pull himself out should he fall through. This is how he set off from the landing. Each time he took a step, he tested the way before him. Although this process was necessary, it made the way very slow.

After spending most of the morning testing the ice each step of the way, and having crossed nearly three-quarters of the way, George let his guard down. Stepping on what appeared to be solid ice without testing it, George put his foot through. In an instant, he could feel the chill of winter water pressing his pant leg tight against his knee. In another instant, his foot was back on firm ice, but the cold water was working its way down the calf of his boot and soaking through the eyelets at the foot.

The picture of Ruth bent over her bread came to mind: "Don't come back wet." He wouldn't really be wet by the time he got back home;

he would be frozen from foot to knee. Keeping on to the post office to save his pride was not an option, though. That walk, plus the way back home, would be too far to travel with what was quickly going to become a frozen foot.

George looked up at the hazy winter sun barely making itself known through the low clouds that hung over the bay. Judging from its position, by the time he got home Ruth would be serving dinner anyway. With his foot getting colder by the minute, the prospect of a hot noon meal made George's decision that much easier, so he turned around and tried to the best of his memory to retrace his steps—this time testing every one first.

Ruth was at the stove serving up dinner for the children when she heard George at the door. Since she'd been half expecting him with the mail by this time, there was a place set at the table. Without missing a beat, she picked up another plate and heaped out more steaming stew with a big dumpling on the side.

"That was a quick trip." She hadn't yet glanced up.

"Depends on how you look at it." George brushed past her and, instead of sitting at the table as she expected, pulled his rocking chair up close to the stove and began removing his now-frozen boot.

Not one for "I-told-you-so's," Ruth sat the stew on a warming ledge and bent down to help her husband out of his icy footwear.

"You'd better get out of those pants, too, before you catch cold."

In another hour, dinner was finished and George was sufficiently warmed up to make another try at the crossing. He had almost reached the mainland when he felt the ice beneath his rear foot give way as he moved forward. He turned back to test the spot with his pole. It went right through. Had he lingered there, even for an instant, George would have gone through, too. He made it to the mainland warm and dry, but he was still learning that a trip across the ice would never be entirely over until he stood on solid ground.

When George got to the post office, about an hour's walk from the breakwater, there was a full week's worth of mail waiting: correspondence from his superiors, corrected homework assignments—plus new ones—for Thelma, Rosa, Malcolm, and Minna, letters from Ruth's family and George's sisters, the weekly installment of the Antigonish *Casket*, along with a week's worth of the *Morning Chronicle* that David Sutton had left for George to pick up. All of this made for quite a load to carry back home, and as George began his return trip, he remembered the hole he'd left in the ice just as he stepped ashore. How was he going to get across on ice this poor with the added weight of the mail?

> *On two different occasions I crossed the ice with the horse in the afternoon and came out the next morning to see open water.*
> *—George Millar*

He was turning this question over in his mind as he walked toward the Bayfield wharf. As his eyes came to rest on the old board fence that lined the road, his memory flashed back to the rain-soaked battlefields of France and Belgium, where the troops had used slatted duck boards to create walkways over the mud in the trenches.

Why not try the same thing on the ice? The fence boards could distribute his weight over a larger area and make his crossing safer. Technically, George supposed it would be stealing or vandalism, but he could put the boards back in place soon enough. Right now, he had an emergency. Accordingly, he selected two broad boards from the fence and made his crossing by laying one on the ice, walking to its end, and placing the other board down at the end of the first. This he repeated until he reached land. Back home in the warmth of his kitchen, George was congratulating himself on his ingenuity when he was struck by another inspiration: Why not rig up a pair of skis?

The first pair was a crude replica of the real thing: made from pieces of wide board, sharpened at the front ends, and fastened to the feet by homemade leather straps. But they served the purpose until George was able to obtain thin strips of hardwood to take into his workshop and fashion a proper pair. For added insurance on poor ice, these skis were wider and shorter than conventional ones, and they saw George safely across for many years.

These homemade conveyances earned George a measure of renown among his mainland cronies. This regard—whether for the nerve or the foolhardiness that found a man on ice no one else in his right mind would step on—could sometimes be heard expressed as "Millar will cross on a heavy dew."

George's confidence on the ice was bolstered by an additional adaptation—an ice boat. His consisted of a lightweight rowboat that he fitted with hardwood runners. These allowed him to row across open water, then push the boat across ice floes to the next patch of water. It was an arduous process that took much longer than the usual half-hour of steady rowing between landing and breakwater. Still, it allowed passage under conditions that would otherwise be impassable.

Maybe George became too cocky about his success outwitting the enemy or maybe it just didn't occur to him that misfortune of any scope could befall him, he who had stared down death many times already. But whether it was hubris or just plain bad luck, the ice came close to claiming both George and Ruth in the winter of 1948.

They were on their way home across the frozen water and, for the second time, Ruth felt the ice give way under her left foot. The first dip into the bay had barely topped her winter boot so George didn't make much of it.

"I'm wet to the knee now," she said.

She wasn't sure if it was the blood in her leg or the winter stocking under her dress that was freezing. Maybe he would believe her this time.

"Don't be foolish, woman, you couldn't be. Not with fourteen inches of ice."

George urged Ruth onward. She was getting colder by the minute, but it was no use complaining to her husband. She kept walking. "Well, it's so anyway."

George had to have the last word. "Impossible!"

They had been walking arm-in-arm for about half an hour across the frozen bay between the breakwater and the Pomquet Island landing.

With every step George would test the ice ahead using his stick. The night was clear now, but the sudden winter storm that had stranded them at the wharf had also blown away the small trees George always arranged across the unbroken white to mark safe passage.

The moon was so bright they could see their shadows. Fresh, glittering snow had drifted into an undulating pattern of shade and light as far across the bay as the eye could see. They could almost feel the silence. It was like a vacuum after the howling winds and whipping snow that had kept them holed up in the lobster cannery office for two hours. This had come at the end of a harrowing drive from Glen Alpine, where Minna had recently begun teaching school. Now it was time to go home. David and Barbara had been alone long enough.

George opened his mouth to give Ruth more reasons why the ice was perfectly solid. Before he could even draw a breath, the ice gave way and they both crashed through. George was back up almost as soon as he was down, but in the stumble, they'd let go of each other.

George looked wildly for Ruth, and it was as close to panic as he would ever be. Only her torso was out of the water. The rest was wedged under the ice behind her. She was clawing with all her strength, trying to pull herself out of the dark, frigid hole. But even as she did so, Ruth could feel her coat and boots begin to pull her down. She tried to kick her legs, but the cold was making it hard to move.

"Take my hands!" George grabbed around her wrists and pulled with all his might. She moved a few inches toward him, but the thick ice weighing on her backside had a tight grip. He pulled again. This time, she came a little farther out. Finally in desperation, George stood up, grasped Ruth under her arms, and pulled upward with all his might. He fell backward and she fell on top of him, dripping and shivering.

They helped each other up and began to assess the damage. Ruth's clothes were quickly freezing. If she didn't get moving right away, she might not be able to. Already her feet were numb. George twirled slowly in place and surveyed the unbroken tranquility that surrounded them.

Already, wisps of snow were drifting across a thin membrane beginning to form over the hole. If there were rifts caused by the pressure of wind and sea on the ice of the bay, George and Ruth might never see them. The snow would already have covered them.

"Where could they be?" David was just reaching the bottom of the stairs and heading for the dining room to join Barbara. She'd been curled up in the rocker by the stove all evening, well tucked into a good, solid adventure with the Bobbsey Twins. David was returning from his third visit that night to the lantern room. He'd been using it as a vantage point to scan the bay for sight of his parents. "They must be storm-stayed somewhere."

Thirteen-year-old Barbara was enjoying the bright light of the Aladdin lamp hanging above the dining room table. She didn't look up.

"We're not supposed to burn this for so long." David reached to turn down the flame. At seventeen, he was the oldest at home now and therefore in charge.

"Wait! Let me finish this chapter!"

"Don't take too long. We'll be in trouble if we use too much kerosene. Mum and Dad will know we've been up late, too."

Barbara looked up for the first time since her older brother had entered the room. "What time is it anyway?"

"Midnight. Guess we'd better let the fire go out, too."

David lifted the lid on the stove and peered inside. The smallest pieces from the last load of wood were long gone, and the largest were mostly embers now, licked only around their ends by bright orange flame.

"Okay." Barbara resented the intrusion into her story. "Just give me five minutes."

"All right, but you never know when they could come in the door."

"Thought you didn't see anything…" The absent quality in Barbara's voice said she was still more engrossed in her book than the conversation.

"Yeah, but that doesn't mean they aren't on their way. It just means I didn't see them."

Knowing that his sister wasn't much interested in him or any subject other than the Bobbsey Twins, David trucked back upstairs and changed into his pyjamas before climbing up to the cold third storey again for one more look. There was no light to tend this time of the year; winter shipping had long since ceased on St. George's Bay. Sometime during the 1940s, the lantern began closing down at the end of November after the last of the local fishing boats were hauled up for the season. George followed the lead of the keeper at Henry Island to the northeast. When that lamp went dark for the winter, so did Pomquet Island's.

As he had done several times before on this evening, David scanned the harbour. Without the inside light for interference, he was impressed by how clearly he could see the features of the Bayfield shoreline lit by the bright, white moon. The ice looked smooth and calm, except for the huge hills that pushed up onto the Pomquet Island shore in the gale that had just passed. The angle of his sight didn't quite allow him to see his parents crossing from the breakwater, but there was still some satisfaction in the looking. Now that he was the only boy at home, David spent a lot of time helping his father travel back and forth to the mainland in all kinds of weather, and he, more than Barbara, knew how treacherous the ice could be.

By 1948, David and Barbara were the only Millar children still remaining on Pomquet Island. Rosa, who had left the island in the summer of 1940, was married and had already started a family of her own. Thelma, who had left for nursing school in the winter of 1941, was working at the Kentville Sanatorium. Malcolm, who had joined the Royal Canadian Air Force during World War II, had taken advantage of an opportunity for ex-servicemen and was studying forestry at the University of New Brunswick. Minna, meanwhile, had just begun a teaching career in Glen Alpine, not far from Antigonish. It was from here that George and Ruth were returning when the snowstorm struck.

And quite a storm it was. The winds were strong enough to shake the square, white lighthouse on its foundation. Still, with the exception of a small amount of snow that had sifted through the corners of the plate glass in the lantern house, everything had held up. Of course, the upstairs was colder than usual because the wind had made the drafts that much stronger, and there was frost inside all the north- and east-facing windows, both upstairs and down. But it was not the first time any of these things had happened.

David reckoned the five minutes he had given Barbara were more than up by now, so he turned from the window and headed down the lantern stairs. As he came to the top of the steps in the main house, he called out a warning to his sister:

"Okay! It's time for bed now. Better turn off the lamp and put the book away."

Barbara was already out of the chair and sticking a spare piece of kindling in the stove for a flame to light a second lamp when David arrived in the dining room.

"Let's leave a light on in case they come home while it's still dark."

David took his job of being in charge seriously, but he was humble enough to allow that his sister may be right. "Good idea. We'll leave it here on the table."

Normally, a burning lamp wouldn't be left untended in the house, but these were special circumstances, and the flame would be kept very low.

David pulled down on the Aladdin lamp, which was suspended over the table by a pulley apparatus. After turning down the flame until it extinguished, David pushed the lamp back up to its normal position near the ceiling. He lit a third lamp, then, the one he and Barbara would use to see their way upstairs to their beds. Once there, he waited until his younger sister had burrowed deep under the cold covers before setting the lamp on the floor outside his bedroom door, extinguishing the flame and diving into his own bed.

There were very few occasions when George Millar wasn't sure of himself, but this moment on the deceitful ice, halfway between

Bayfield and Pomquet Island, was one of them. A misstep in any direction could be his last one.

"What now?"

He didn't realize he had spoken aloud until he heard Ruth reply.

"Well, we know what's behind us and we don't want to go through that again. We don't know what's ahead. It may be better. I say we go forward."

The words were remarkably cogent coming from a woman who, by now, could barely move her numb legs under frozen clothes. This time, George gave some weight to what she had to say. So they shuffled on again, this time at arm's-length, facing and gripping each other by both hands. This way, if one of them fell through, it was more likely the other could keep them both from going under. It was painstaking progress now, because with each step George would have to break his grip on Ruth, stretch out his pole to test the ice, then take his wife's hands once again. Even with these precautions, Ruth broke through two more times. By now, though, she was numb to the waist and barely counted her stumbles.

> *On we went slowly,*
> *with a pole I carried in*
> *my hand. Every step*
> *a prayer, every minute*
> *an eternity.*
> *—George Millar*

It took a good hour of creeping sideways, testing the ice ahead, grasping hands, and taking a few more steps, before the two came close to the island. When they did, they saw that their way was barred by tall hummocks of ice, pushed into the shallows and onto the shore. They had been so busy looking for safe footing, they hadn't examined their horizon.

"You wait here. I'll see if I can find an easy route to the shore."

George left Ruth standing on the ice, frozen stiff and shivering, afraid to move one step to the right or the left, while he scouted the easiest path to land. He was back within five minutes, but to Ruth it felt like an eternity. "Found it!"

Even after clambering over giant chunks of ice and scrambling over rubble, there was still the half-hour walk to the lighthouse along a snow-buried track. But that would be easy. At least they could put one foot in front of the other without worrying about whether they were going to go down. Eventually they could see the warm, yellow glow of a light from the dining room window. It was somewhere near 2:00 A.M. The kitchen stove had long ago sputtered out, but there was still some warmth in the house.

As soon as they got inside, George loaded up the kitchen stove with more wood while Ruth pried off her frozen clothing. After opening the oven door, they brought a chair up to the stove, and Ruth spent the next two hours with her legs wrapped in bath towels and resting on the oven door. George, having completed the adventure with one iced-up foot, was close by. Without speaking, they clasped hands by the warmth of the stove and silently offered prayers of thanks to the Master Pilot. It was a night they would not soon forget, and it called for two cups of strong, hot tea.

By morning, both George and Ruth were sufficiently warmed up to resume their normal duties. Immediately after breakfast, George set off to the landing searching for the cause of the previous night's treachery. He scaled a likely looking pile of ice, and from this vantage point could see a great rift in the thick winter ice between the mainland and the island. The wind and high seas had pushed the solid pack of bay ice toward the breakwater so that it wedged open a large crack extending almost the full distance from breakwater to island. Because the night had been cold, a thin skin of new ice formed quickly and the snow had drifted over it. Had George and Ruth chosen to walk even a little more to the west, they would have fallen through the gap.

George restored the small spruce saplings marking the safest route between island and breakwater. The whole family understood that unsafe ice was one of the hazards of lightkeeping life, so there would be no dwelling on what

It may seem strange to a person not familiar with such conditions that a person would walk into open fissures in the ice. But in sub-zero weather with drifting snow, a thin film quickly forms over small patches of open water; thus, good and bad ice look alike.
—George Millar

might have happened. Life would go on the way it always had. It wasn't as if there was a choice. Ruth's legs had been frozen from toe to hip, but she would cross on the ice many more times that winter and many winters after that. Each time, she would do her best not to think back to the night that both the water and the cold had tried to claim her.

If Ruth had wanted mollycoddling after her close call, she knew George would not be the person to look to. Her husband had little patience with people who asked for special attention, and Ruth had a good idea why. As a youthful soldier, he had taken injuries in stride and brushed elbows with death more than once. The balm for George's troubles had been that he got out alive.

Ruth knew, too, that George's hardness was sometimes hurtful to his children. He demanded much of them, but no more than he demanded of himself. She could see that he had mellowed over the years, though. If she gave the reasons some thought, she might have been able to trace it back to Vimy—not George's first time there fighting in the mud and the rain, but the second time, when she and George had gone back together in the summer of 1936.

Back then she knew the sights, the sounds, the fear, and the unimaginable hell of the front were still with George, and that he needed to get them out. So Ruth paid close heed to news of the Vimy Memorial as it slowly took shape on a high ridge in France. She was as relieved as anyone when George received an invitation from the Royal Canadian Legion to go to France for the monument's unveiling in July 1936. Money was scarce, but money would be found for this trip.

The Vimy Pilgrimage was cause for great excitement in the Millar household. George and Ruth both bought new raincoats in honour of the trip, and Ruth made a brand new navy blue suit to wear. This would be the first time the parents left their children for more than a night at a time; after all, Baby Barbara was still barely eighteen months old. George's sister Annie and her husband Aubrey made the journey from

Pugwash to the island with their three children to watch the light and their nieces and nephews.

No one—except George, perhaps—was more proud than Ruth to stand in the crowd of one hundred thousand on Vimy Ridge and watch King Edward VIII pull back the drape that had concealed the stone monument—a female image of "Canada mourning for her dead." Like six thousand other Canadians, George and Ruth also had the chance to explore the old battlefield, where George could still name some of the craters the constant shelling had created. Like the other pilgrims, they strolled through the cemeteries where so many of George's comrades-in-arms lay buried.

Ruth had had an inkling of how the war had shaped her husband's character. Now she knew. Having joined up at age eighteen, George had come into manhood on the battlefield. The infantry was his family, and its customs were his. There had been no way out. He had lived in the mire, and blood, and stench, and unholy noise. And somehow, he had survived.

Tours of the old battlefields in France and Belgium helped close George's old wounds and renew his gratitude for the home he now had on Pomquet Island. As for his children, they reveled in the benevolence of their Uncle Aubrey's rule. For the first time in her life, Rosa did not worry about being "painted green and let run" as a way for her father to save on summer clothing. Malcolm had a taste of new pleasures, driving with Uncle Aubrey in his father's Model A, windows rolled down, radio blaring. And they all had three cousins to include in their play. But the older Millar children knew, even as they watched their uncle do it, that the carving of his initials into a supporting beam in the barn would be worthy of something like a court marshal when George found out.

> *It was much easier to realize just what our boys actually did endure. I could picture them clogging along, foot-sore and weary, and then coming to the abrupt ascent of the ridge. How it must have taken every ounce of reserve energy to make it!*
> —*Ruth Millar*

Her parents had been away from Pomquet Island for nearly five weeks when Thelma woke in the night to a sound coming from the dining room below. It sounded like a window was being opened. She propped herself onto her elbows and stretched her neck to look about and listen. There it was again: a bump, scuffle, and scrape.

No one else seemed to have heard it. Rosa continued in unbroken sleep next to her, and there was no sound from Malcolm and David's room, nor from Minna and Barbara's bed in a curtained area of the upstairs hall. Then came a muffled thud against the floor downstairs, and what sounded like a window being raised or lowered in its sash.

Careful not to jar her sleeping sister, fourteen-year-old Thelma slid out of bed and tiptoed down the hall past the master bedroom where Aunt Annie and Uncle Aubrey slept, too weary from keeping track of nine children to hear bumps in the night. This must have been why her uncle had locked the doors at bedtime, something her own parents never did.

Thelma tried to miss the squeaky parts of the stairs as she hurried to investigate. Moonlight from a clear summer night streamed in two windows and gave the dining room a fuzzy, grey glow. As she entered the room Thelma recognized the form of her father by the window. Without a word, he reached out and pulled her to him, cradling her head against his chest. Thelma held her breath. It seemed like forever, and when he finally released the embrace she shook her head to clear it. It had been a long time since Thelma had been held in her father's arms. She had long ago accepted the family convention that demonstrating affection to a child older than six was overdoing it.

But, to George, this one time was not at all excessive—it was simply thanks to the Master Pilot.

*We would sometimes find an empty on the shore below
the light. Coincidence? Did it come from a passing boat?
Or was the "dead soldier" thrown in the hope that it
would sink from sight?* —Malcolm Millar

Growing Pains

CHAPTER EIGHT

*I*f she had taken the time to reflect upon it, Ruth would have connected the new hollow feeling in her stomach with George bringing home the *Morning Chronicle* every day. It was June of 1938, and the couple's memories of the Vimy Pilgrimage were passing into the warm fadedness of oilcloth on a sunny, well-trodden floor. But now there was a lengthening shadow cast by more talk of war. Soon, Ruth would be dreading the mail, too.

George had remained in the militia after his discharge at the end of World War I. He and Ruth hadn't spoken of it yet, but both knew he would be called up again. At age thirty-nine, it wasn't likely he would see the front lines, but the thought of any type of war service had a way of making one's stomach churn. And it did not look as if there were a way out—either for George or for his country. Adolf Hitler was well into his program of isolating and eradicating Jews. Just two months earlier his armies had annexed Austria, and now he was turning his sights to Czechoslovakia and Poland.

There was a momentary bright spot on this side of the Atlantic, though, and it centred on a world heavyweight boxing title match. American Joe Louis and German Max Schmeling were about to fight at Yankee Stadium in New York City. To all of North America and Germany, these two men symbolized the fight between the free world and the Nazis. Max Schmeling was hailed by Hitler as the archetype of Aryan superiority, while in America, Joe Louis was the very embodiment of freedom and the American Dream. For Louis, the reigning champion, this fight would be his chance to erase any doubts that he deserved the crown. If he could knockout Schmeling, as the latter had done to him two years earlier, Louis would put paid to the man who had broken his unbeaten streak. For Schmeling, it was a chance to regain the title he had held briefly from 1930–1931.

When they weren't speculating about whether—or when—Canada would go to war, everyone on the mainland was talking about the fight. There was lots of hype. Some claimed Schmeling planned to use the fight purse to help build more tanks for his country's war effort. Others had heard it said that a black man could not beat a German. The ire over this kind of talk reverberated to the very ends of the fishing wharves of the nation.

And George Millar was in the middle of it all. Being a veteran of The Great War meant he carried a certain weight with his friends. Not only was he able to discuss the latest reports in the daily newspaper, but he could also tell his cronies what he'd heard on his radio, one of few in the area. So, as the June 22 boxing bout approached, a few of George's friends made plans to row over to the island and listen firsthand.

One thing the Millar children rarely saw their father do was drink, and liquor never did cross the threshold of the Pomquet Island lighthouse. Still, there was little doubt much of the anticipation for the Louis–Schmeling fight was sweetened by the knowledge that there would be something to drink with more kick than the usual strong morning tea. Sometimes, after George had hosted a mainland friend on the island, the children would find an empty bottle here or there. Anticipating the fight of the century, the fishermen were rightly expecting some of the same hospitality.

On the night of the fight, the men brought some of their own liquor along for sipping during brief breaks outside, and they could not resist sampling it on the way across the water. Now, in the mood for putting their patriotic ears to the moment-by-moment commentary of the Louis–Schmeling fight, this ragtag band of men swaggered toward George and Ruth Millar's back porch in the gathering dusk.

"Sorry, boys!" The men were barely out of the woods when they saw George silhouetted in the doorway calling across the yard. "Fight's over!"

"Waddya mean, over?" challenged George's militia buddy, Bert Cameron. "It's barely even time for it to start!" He made it to the door first and was now squinting at George from the bath of light cast by the open door. Bert was finding the news difficult to comprehend. For one reason, his mind wasn't working as quickly as it otherwise might, and for another, he knew George had been looking forward to a few shots from the nearly-full bottle of Seagram's Bert was cradling inside his jacket.

Bert's mainland partners were beginning to catch up, one at a time straggling out of the bush-shaded track from the landing. "Over ya say?" David Sutton had only just stopped to take a swig from Jack Randall's proffered mickey. Now he was panting from the exertion of catching up to the others. "Waddya mean, over?"

"I just asked that question, myself, Dave, bye," came the word from Cameron, who was himself reaching into his breast pocket for something to take away the sting of George's words.

George closed the porch door behind him and took a step into the warm June night. "Yep. It's over. In two minutes. Joe Louis knocked him cold!"

"Well I'll be…" It was Herbie Chisholm bringing up the rear, a bit unsteady on his feet. They were all having trouble registering what George was saying.

The mainlanders had set off at what they thought was an early hour, but they had misjudged how long it would take to get from the landing to the house when drinks were included in the trek. Meanwhile, George had tuned in to the fight at the appointed hour and sat down to listen to the preliminaries, confident his friends would be along shortly. He was unconcerned when the fight got underway with his cronies still absent. There would be lots of time. It had taken Louis eight rounds to win the title he now held, and it had taken Schmeling twelve to beat Louis before that. There would probably be a chance for the group of them to step outside and hang around the well for a while. That was where George liked to take a drink or two with his friends—where they could cut the strong taste with fresh water if need be, and where they could toss an empty or two over the bank unobserved.

Tonight, though, Louis pinned Schmeling to the ropes at the opening bell and never let him recover. Louis was victorious after just two minutes and four seconds. Schmeling had gotten off only two punches. George's friends were as glad as anyone for the symbolic victory over the German, but none could disguise his disappointment at not being there to hear it, and at being robbed of a good long evening's jawing and drinking.

I recall a day during haying season when the MacKinnons were visiting the island. Angus and Dad spent some time at the well where we got our drinking water for household use. I think the well water was not being taken straight.
—Malcolm Millar

"All right, boys!" Bert raised his arms high in front of him as though he were herding cattle. "We might as well git goin'. It's a long way home."

"It's awful early to be goin' home." Herbie lowered himself unsteadily onto a splitting block that stood next to the woodshed. He was trying to reach into his jacket pocket but his hand kept missing the opening. "Why don't we have a little visit before we go?"

The others began to murmur agreement and look around for places to rest. George gave no response. Bert was the only one sharp enough to notice his friend's silence, so he raised his arms again. "Git goin', the lot a yus! Missus Millar doesn't want a bunch a galoots hangin' around in her yard with the little ones upstairs tryin' ta git ta sleep."

There were some muttered curses as the men turned themselves around and made their way toward the woods. George stood in the doorway watching the shadowy figures fade back into the track from whence they'd come. He stayed there for a while after they'd disappeared, enjoying the warm June night. Now and then he would catch a burst of profanity or laughter rising from the trees as his friends gradually made their way back to the landing.

> *I was upstairs in bed [even for a thirteen-year-old, the curfew was 7:30 P.M.] and recall overhearing through the open window some disappointed oaths as they departed in disgust in the darkness.*
> *—Malcolm Millar*

George Millar was never heard by a member of his family to utter a swear word. Despite coming through the hell of the trenches in World War I, and despite spending his days off the island mostly in the company of hard-working fishermen or hardened Army reservists, the worst George could be heard to say was something like "Gol' darn," or, when the end was surely nigh for an almost-swamped rowboat, "God save us!"

In this respect and others, the island existence was a sheltered one. So on a fine July day little more than a year after the famous boxing bout, Malcolm was reveling in some new-found independence as he surveyed the hayfield. He contemplated the fuzzy heads of ripe hay waving in the light breeze, tossing back and forth like a million little tails rolling in unison. The motion began where field met barnyard and swelled along to the lip of the cliff, giving the effect of hay reaching all the way to the horizon. Only a gannet gliding high on an air current made a mark on the clear blue sky.

"Today's the day," he said.

The hayfield was bordered on one side by barnyard, on two sides by a high bank, and on the other by the spruce woods that covered most of the island. It was somewhere near ten o'clock in the morning, and the hay had already lost its overnight moisture. Warm July sun cloaked Malcolm's shoulders. He pinched a waist-high stalk of green just below its head and pulled. Then he clamped its juicy root end between his teeth and savoured the straw-sweet flavour. It was perfect for mowing. As he chewed, he considered where to begin. There was a feeling of luxury in the choosing: for the first time in months, the young man was out from under his father's thumb.

"You'll need to get that hay in this week if it stays fine," were George's last words to his eldest son as he took the gunny sack Malcolm was passing up from the rowboat.

"Yes, sir," came the automatic response.

Then, conscious his father was watching, Malcolm—just barely fourteen—manoeuvred the boat away from the breakwater and began to row in the direction of home.

That was yesterday, and George would be staying on the mainland for the rest of the week. Malcolm had dropped him off so he could break the family car out of storage and drive it to Antigonish where he would join his militia buddies for summer exercises over the next four days. With both Thelma and Rosa on the mainland for the summer—Thelma housekeeping for the McChesneys in Afton and Rosa housekeeping for her grandparents in Pugwash—Malcolm was the oldest child on the island. David would spend most of the day stacking summer-dried firewood inside the porch to make a winter's supply. Minna, Malcolm's junior by four years, and Barbara, who was only five, would likely put some time into the potato patch picking bugs. That left Ruth to tend the light and Malcolm in charge of the farming.

"Today's the day," Malcolm repeated, because there was satisfaction in the repetition. It bespoke the confidence of a seasoned farmer. If he started now, he could get in two good hours before Mum called him in for dinner.

"We gonna mow today?" David, seven years old, was out of breath, eager, and bringing up the rear. He was a small lad, slighter and darker than his big brother. David's hair and skin favoured his father, but his eyes had a hazel colour, somewhere between his father's brown and his mother's blue. After a summer spent outdoors barefoot in short pants, he had the kind of swarthy look that a sailor picks up over a season on the high seas. Malcolm had a summer tan, too, but he wore long pants, his hair was a bit lighter, and his eyes were blue. He was tall enough that he could look down at the top of his younger brother's head. "That's right."

The decision to cut hay had been an easy one for Malcolm, given that the day had dawned just as fine and dry as the two before. There was no rain in the forecast, but for confirmation he looked northwest toward Cape George and back inland in the direction of Antigonish. He could see no cloud or foreboding in either direction, and it was the same as far he could make out to the east over Cape Breton in the hazy distance.

Imitating his big brother's mature posture, David broke off a piece of hay and placed it in his mouth. With a hand still on the seed end, he followed his brother's gaze. "Weather's gonna be fine for a while."

"Should be." Malcolm pulled the mangled green stalk from his teeth and discarded it on the ground, as he'd often seen his father do, then strode toward the pasture. David did the same thing and followed, shouting "C'mon, Don!" as he put on a burst of speed and raced ahead of his brother.

Don was the big buckskin horse who, until now, had been grazing mildly in a small pasture alongside the family's two milk cows. Now he looked up and pricked his ears toward the familiar voice. He took a couple of steps toward the boys as they closed the distance.

"Time to cut some hay, boy."

David reached up for it, but Malcolm grabbed Don's oversized halter first and began leading the horse toward the barn. David walked alongside. As soon as Don stepped into the dark and cool of the small building, he raised his head high, stretching Malcolm's arm along with it. He knew something was up. Malcolm turned him around in the alley as barefoot David skitted out of the way. The horse shifted his weight a few times, moving his feet and nodding cheerfully to show he was ready for whatever was coming next.

In this respect Don was different from Jumbo, whose old age had claimed him a few years earlier. The huge and plodding grey was remembered for having the patience of Job and the stance of a sphinx. A child could climb all over Jumbo from nose to tail and he wouldn't move a muscle. The old plug would just stand there, neck and head down low, heavy-lidded eyes blinking benignly, his ears shifting now and then. But the memory of Jumbo had dimmed in the year or two since his demise. Don was the horse of the day now, and with him came a new set of habits to get used to.

David had already climbed partly up a stable wall to take down the heavy leather collar that was Jumbo's legacy to his successor. He passed it to Malcolm, and Don knew what was next. He didn't need to be asked to lower his head for Malcolm to slip the oval-shaped appliance around his neck.

"Here you go, boy."

The collar did not fit as snugly on the new horse as it had on the old one, but it was serviceable enough. Don waited, sometimes stamping a foot to rid a leg of flies, while Malcolm and David sorted out the bridle. It was large, and it had blinders that would keep him from being surprised by anything approaching from the sides or behind. At the sound of the tack jingling, Don opened his great, toothy mouth even before Malcolm had readied the bit.

As the young man slipped the bridle over Don's ears and snugged it around his bony jaws, the horse shook his massive head and neck with a gusto that almost knocked Malcolm over.

"Jeepers, Don!"

The boy had expected this, although it always seemed to catch him off guard. He never knew exactly when the horse was going to get him with this earth-moving shake. This one caused Malcolm to stagger a bit.

"Holy cow!"

David didn't say whether he was impressed by Don's power or Malcolm's ability to withstand it. In either case, he climbed onto a bench to reach for the reins while Malcolm righted himself. With the shake completed, Don was content to stand patiently now, waiting for the remainder of his harness. Once Malcolm satisfied himself that all the gear was in place, he led Don around the barn to the hay mower.

"Back up, boy."

Malcolm stood in front of the animal and urged him backwards between two long wooden shafts that would fit into the harness strapped to Don's back.

"How many horsepower do you figure Don has?"

David was helping to guide a shaft into position along the horse's side. Malcolm was on the other side doing the same thing.

"Don't know."

Chain traces attached to Don's collar would pull the mower, a machine with a long, saw-toothed blade that could be raised or lowered. The blade was connected to an axle that held together two large, iron wheels. As the wheels turned with the horse's pulling, the blade moved back and forth to cut the hay.

"Must be at least two," hazarded David. Then he jumped clear because he knew what was coming. As soon as Don felt the weight of the mower distributed through the harness on his back, he took a step forward.

"Whoa, Don. Not yet, boy. Wait 'til I get behind."

Don hadn't pulled anything since he had hauled the plow nearly three months ago, and he was eager to get started. Conscious of the horse's keenness, Malcolm reached for the reins, now resting on Don's back. Holding them high in one hand, he moved quickly to the mower and climbed into the iron seat mounted between the wheels on the axle. David looked on with brotherly envy. His legs were not yet long enough for this job.

"Giddup, boy!"

Malcolm hardly needed to say the words. Don was already leaning into the load.

Malcolm kept the blade high while David followed a bit behind and to the right. Malcolm steered the horse to the treed edge of the hayfield. His path was just outside the perimeter of lessening morning shade, where he could be sure the hay was dry. Malcolm lowered the boom, and the familiar scrape, slice, and clank of summer mowing began. From his high seat, he could see the tall greenness fall flat before the blades and feel startled grasshoppers clashing against his legs. Seagulls picked up quickly on the earthly commotion and began to congregate overhead, then swoop down to pluck new treasures uncovered by the mower. Their sudden dives and takeoffs were shielded from the horse by his blinders, so his path from barnyard to cliff edge and back was undisturbed.

Malcolm hadn't noticed David drop back and turn in the direction of the house. He was busy watching the blade. It was a dangerous thing. He still remembered Stumpy the rabbit from last summer. Stumpy had not been swift enough to hop out of the path of the coming mower before he lost a front leg.

George had used the occasion to reinforce a message to his children: "Step in front of the mower when there's a horse hitched to it, and that's what'll happen to you."

George and the children had brought the injured rabbit home, where he was given a name and placed inside a custom-built cage. Stumpy had long ago returned to the wild by now, but his progeny might still be slow enough for a repeat accident. Malcolm was vigilant, though, and everything was well in hand. He relaxed a bit more into the cool, metal seat.

Don's buckskin coat gleamed golden in the sun, and Malcolm could see it ripple now and then to shift horseflies and grasshoppers. The horse's black tail had settled into a constant sweeping motion to fend off newly disturbed bugs, and he would nod his head periodically or shake his black-maned neck to rid his face and ears of insects. But Malcolm didn't need to ask Don to keep moving on. He was bending his body to the work, glad to be of service.

As he relaxed into his seat, letting the reins rest flat in his hands, Malcolm inhaled the sweet freshness of new-mown hay, and felt the warm sun on his face. This was the life! And it was all Malcolm's, all day today.

"D-i-i-n-n-er!"

The voice came from far away and didn't register at first.

"Mal-colm! Din-ner t-i-i-me!"

It was David sent to singsong his older brother home to eat. Malcolm jerked back into the present. He had drifted off after all, even as he watched the mower blade closely. No harm done, though. He waved to show David he'd heard and finished cutting a swath from the cliff to the barnyard. David met horse and driver there, where they unhitched the horse and relieved him of his bridle. Don was left with water to drink and grass to eat while the boys went in for dinner.

The others were already waiting at the table when Malcolm and David entered the house. Their sisters watched them come in while their mother began dishing out food from where she sat at the table.

Ruth looked up. "Brush some of that chaff off before you come and sit down."

Malcolm stepped back outside and beat his hands over his head and shoulders. Returning to the scene in the dining room, he felt a rush of pride. Today he felt like the guest of honour. Usually, it was his father everyone waited for at the table. Malcolm was the man of the house today, and that felt good, although he did not allow his face to betray him. Instead, he took his customary place at the table and waited for his plate.

As usual, at dinnertime the air was filled with chatter, but Malcolm was not inclined to contribute much to the conversation himself. It was mostly the younger ones keeping up the buzz, speculating on how many potato bugs they might capture and how many sticks of wood David could carry in one go. Their mother remained mostly quiet, too, simply nodding now and then to encourage the others.

With dinner finished, David and Malcolm hitched the horse and mower for the afternoon's work. As the sun began its slow descent from the noon sky, Minna and Barbara helped their mother clear the table and wash the dishes before heading to the potato patch. David returned reluctantly to the firewood, and Malcolm lowered the mower blade again.

It was Don who felt it first but, like Malcolm behind him, he did not register what was happening. Don was just at the end of another row, swinging around to the right on a "Gee, Don," from Malcolm, when something moved underneath him. For a moment he felt light, then heavy as a boulder, as the ground beneath his feet gave way completely. Before he had a chance to be afraid, or to shy to the side, Don was falling, tumbling, churning. Red sand was skidding into his eyes and nose and mouth. Rocks were bouncing off his hide and sliding underneath him.

Malcolm didn't have time to bail out. As soon as Don disappeared over the bank, the shafts of the mower, held firmly in the harness, upended the whole machine and pitched it forward. Malcolm felt himself sailing through the air, past a bird's-eye view of his tumbling horse's underbelly, and smack into a deep bed of old seaweed, now dry and buzzing with flies in the sun.

It took him a few seconds to reorient himself. His shoulder was sore where he'd landed, but as far as he could tell, nothing was broken. He looked himself over. Except for a scrape on his knee, there was no blood. He wiped a forearm across his nose to be sure. The mower was scattered in pieces along the rocky shore. Both shafts lay shattered nearby. The blade, which had become detached from the machine, was lying bent on the rocks farther down the beach. Only the axle and wheels kept their former shape where they had rolled to a stop near the water.

Behind him, Malcolm heard a groan. It was Don, collar still around his neck but screwed sideways. He was upright at least, but lying on his belly, front legs splayed out in front of him, rocking back and forth, pushing with his front hooves. He was trying to get up but was caught in a tangle of harness. As soon as Don had dropped over the cliff, the long reins had whipped from Malcolm's hands and trailed after the horse. Now they were wound around his body, keeping him from stretching his neck to its full length so he could get himself up.

"Easy, boy." Malcolm scrambled to the animal's aid. "Stay still while I get you free."

He stumbled over intractable rocks to Don's head and began undoing the buckles that held the bridle in place, then slipping it off over the horse's ears. As he traced the wrap of the reins and carefully unwound them from Don's barrel, Malcolm eyed some scrapes on the animal's back and legs. There was nothing he could see that wouldn't clean up with a little water and disinfectant. He let out a breath of relief, and Don echoed the sentiment in a blow through his nostrils.

"What happened?"

Malcolm looked up to see David through the freshly torn cliff edge about twenty-five feet above. "Get away from there! It's not safe!"

From this vantage point, Malcolm could see the cause of the upset. No one had walked along this stretch of beach yet this summer, so no one had known that the winter wind and ice had undermined the bank by a good six feet, leaving only a foot-deep chunk of sod overhanging the rocks and beach below. Malcolm could make out last year's grass roots on the underside of the dangling earth. From above, it looked just as solid as ever. From down here, though, the danger was obvious.

There were three faces peering over the edge now, in graduated sizes: Minna's was the largest when you took into account the fringe of curly dark hair that surrounded it. She was the only one of the bunch with her father's brown eyes. David's tanned face and Barbara's blue-eyed visage, framed in blonde hair, were also visible.

"Get back! I mean it! It's dangerous!" All Malcolm needed now was for one of these three to fall over.

"All of you, stay right there!"

They all turned in time to see Ruth sliding through the breach and run-walking down the rocky bank, ignoring for the moment the clay and stones working into her shoes and the mess the brown-red dirt was making of her sky-blue shift.

"Are you all right, Malcolm?" She wasn't even watching where she was stepping. "Are you hurt?"

"No, but I need to get Don up. He's stuck."

Ruth joined Malcolm at Don's head. "David! Bring the halter. Quick!"

At his mother's order, the small lad's face disappeared from the overhang. The two girls left, too, and ran along with him.

Meanwhile, Ruth circled Don, stepping drunkenly over and around the worn, red rocks that were surely causing Don some discomfort. With all the commotion about him, he tried again to get up and groaned again with the strain.

A few minutes later, David called from the overhang and tossed Don's halter onto some rocks nearby. Ruth took it up and slid the gear over his nose and ears. With one matter-of-fact pat to the beast's neck, she stood. "Come on, then, pretty boy. Let's get up."

She tugged on the halter and the horse stretched his nose obligingly toward her while gathering his front legs together. Malcolm scrambled to the rear and tried to lend encouragement with a push to the rump. The big horse raised himself halfway to full height on his front legs, then tried and failed to make his hind legs follow.

"Come along now. You can't stay here."

Ruth was pulling. Malcolm had a shoulder into Don's hind end and was pushing. "Get up, boy!"

"Come on, Don!" came the chorus from above.

With another mighty grunt, the horse scrambled with his back legs to get a purchase on the rocks, then hoisted his rump in one swaying, groaning effort.

"Good boy!"

Everyone said it at once. Minna, Barbara, and David clapped their hands together, and that reminded Ruth to shift her attention upward. "Get away from the edge!"

Assuming the young children would follow their mother's order this time, she returned her attention to the horse and brushed coarse beach sand from his nose and chest.

"Let's get you back home and cleaned up."

Now that he was standing, Don swayed, staggered, and took a tentative step forward. But the ground was covered with sea-worn stones and rubble. The horse was having difficulty finding his legs again. It was low tide, and Ruth tugged the halter in the direction of the water where there would be firmer ground. The horse's first, faltering steps were expected after such a big upset, but by the time he got to the water's edge it was clear there was more to Don's hesitating gait. Malcolm and his mother exchanged looks. The cuts and bruises would heal, but this other injury was an unknown.

"We'll have to take him around to the Seal Rocks and bring him up there."

Ruth was reckoning that would be the closest low point on the bank. But even the rocks the seals used for sunbathing were nearly a quarter of the way around the circumference of the island.

"He's really hurt."

The whole scope of the disaster was beginning to register with Malcolm. His mother nodded but said nothing.

Don kept his head low, except when he drew his right hind foot underneath him. Then the head would bob up, as if someone had goosed him under his tail, which itself stayed clamped to the rear the whole time. One of Don's toes dragged in the sand with every step, so that there was a strange, slithering track behind him.

Malcolm was beginning to calculate the implications of the whole debacle. "Dad's gonna be mad." He had left his feeling of manliness back in the seaweed.

"Not mad, angry." Ruth was concentrating mostly on the horse, and the correction to her son's grammar was automatic, but Malcolm took it as confirmation.

It was a long walk to the barn at the best of times from where horse and driver had landed. With Don's slow and halting gait, it was longer still. By now, the younger children had run ahead along the bank and found a spot where the cliff sloped more gently to the sea. They raced around a headland now to meet the battered party on the beach.

"Here, Don, I brought this for you."

Barbara, barely the height of one of Don's tree-trunk legs, held up a bouquet of purple clover. The horse stopped, nuzzled the offering, and opened his mouth to chew. But even Barbara could see that his heart wasn't in the eating. He let the half-chewed mass fall from his mouth, and the girl let her remaining greenery drop too.

Minna took up an encouraging spot by Don's shoulder on the opposite side from her mother. "Come on home, Don. We'll take care of you."

David had continued running past the horse and his retinue and on to the mower's various parts. Now he came doubling back to report on what he'd seen. "Holy cow! The mower is a total wreck! How are we going to mow the rest of the hay?"

The hay! David was right. Injuring the horse and breaking the mower would be enough in themselves to incur his father's wrath, Malcolm figured. If he let the whole crop of hay go, too, that would be too much. But his mother saved him from figuring out what to do about this.

"You'll have to use the scythe. David and Minna, you two will have to do the raking by hand. Don likely won't be able to pull a rake for awhile."

It took about an hour of encouragement and frequent rest stops to get Don back to the barn. He was hurt, and badly. That was plain. If only he hadn't been so eager to be a man, Malcolm thought to himself. If only he hadn't taken so much pleasure in being out from under his father's glare. This was what he got for being cocky. Who drives a horse over a cliff? Grown men don't do that. George Millar certainly wouldn't do that.

It had been a long time since Malcolm had gotten a waling from his father. The last good one had been over Daisy the cow, and that was four years ago. But this offence couldn't even compare to the previous one. Who knew what George might see as fitting punishment this time?

There was little conversation as they all led Don to his stall, prepared brand new bedding and a clean bucket of water with a treat of oats on the side. To Malcolm, the silence was only further confirmation of his guilt. Only wee Barbara was naïve enough to bring it up at the supper table: "Is Don going to die?"

They all stopped chewing. Malcolm's mouth, which didn't have much in it anyway, went dry. This was the first time the possibility had been raised. David looked from his brother's face to his mother's. Ruth seemed to have her full attention on buttering a piece of bread, and she spoke without looking up. "That's not a question for us to answer." The vigour with which she spread the butter closed the door to further discussion.

Malcolm kept his eyes on his plate and felt the silence. Then Minna stretched to the centre of the table for the milk and turned to her older brother. "Want some?"

But she couldn't single-handedly lift the spirits at the dinner table now. The full weight of Don with his tied-up rear end seemed to sink over the table. No one ate much after that, and Ruth didn't chide anyone for leaving vegetables uneaten. Truth be told, even her food was too cold to be enjoyed by the time she got around to it.

As the day of George's return closed in, Malcolm became more adept at swinging the scythe. By Thursday evening most of the hay was cut, and David and Minna had made a good deal of headway raking by hand. Where there weren't windrows drying in the blessedly continuing sunshine, there were decent-looking stacks of hay. But Don wasn't getting any better.

There was no way to get word to George so that he'd at least be softened up before he got home. There was only telling him after he stepped into the boat when Malcolm picked him up at the breakwater. The lad felt sick just thinking about it. How was he going to tell his father? Whenever he imagined it, Malcolm's tongue felt fuzzy and his gut seemed to drop inside. This must be what guilt felt like. At fourteen, Malcolm had never known the feeling before, because he'd never been given enough leeway to make a decision that he might feel guilty about. His hands were blistered from swinging the scythe, but he kept on, knowing this was precious little payment compared to what he should be giving—or getting.

On Friday, Malcolm was awake with the dawn. As the remnants of the night's clouds burned away in a blaze of gold and pink, he lay in bed listening to his mother's soft footfalls. In the grey light of the house, he heard her pass the room he shared with David, open the door to the lantern stairs, then ascend the steps to extinguish the light. He was already putting the kettle on to boil when his mother arrived in the kitchen ten minutes later.

"You're up early this morning." It was a statement, but his mother phrased it so that it carried a hint of question.

"Need to get the barn work done before I go over to the mainland."

Ruth could hear the muffle in Malcolm's voice that came with not getting enough sleep and being up too early. She kept her voice even and casual. "I thought I'd pick your father up today. It'll give you three more time with the raking. You'll all have to watch Barbara, though."

The cups Malcolm was bringing from the pantry contacted the table in an unusually loud fashion. Ruth noted this but said nothing as she watched her son take his seat with a bit more slump than usual to his shoulders.

"That'll be good. By the time you and Dad get back, we should have it pretty much finished."

Malcolm fixed his eyes on the milk at the centre of the table, but he didn't reach for it. His mind was somewhere else, so his mother passed it to him, and he picked the jug up automatically to pour some white liquid into his cup before his tea. Ruth said nothing further. Instead, she strode to the bottom of the stairs and called for the others to get up. "You've got a lot of work to do today before your father gets home!"

Barbara was the first to notice her parents' return to the island. They were just emerging into the opening at the edge of the woods when she looked that way. The older children were busy forking hay into a tall stack ready for moving from the field to the barn. No one knew yet how that was going to be accomplished with Don laid up.

"Daddy's home!" Barbara—"Bunny" to her father—bounced herself out of a soft spot on another haystack from where she had been watching the work and skipped toward her parents.

George didn't walk to the house with Ruth. He left her to carry his kit bag inside while he made his way to the barn with Bunny was hopping alongside, blonde pigtails bouncing. All three of the older children had kept working, half-looking at their father and half-watching their jobs, then looking again as they saw that he was carrying something none of them had ever seen him carry before.

If war and the coarseness of hand-to-mouth life had turned George from profanity, it had turned him from firearms as well. His children knew he would not allow guns on the island, but he carried one now.

"Is that a rifle?"

David stopped what he was doing to watch his father approach. Malcolm had already taken in what his father had in his hand. "I'd say so."

He continued to fork hay, dreading what was coming next. But David's attention wasn't on the hay anymore. "What's he going to do with that?"

The younger brother kept the fork in his hand and jogged to meet his father. Minna followed, but less in a rush. Malcolm stayed where he was for a moment, still tossing hay. He was getting that feeling again, where his tongue got thick and his stomach sunk.

How Malcolm envied his older sisters! Even if Rosa had not asked to go to Pugwash after her grandmother's stroke, at least she was away from here. And Thelma was on the mainland earning her own money for nursing school, even if it was a job her father told her she had, not one she found herself. Still, they were as good as adults—off Pomquet Island and free. What he wouldn't give to be somewhere else right now. But wishing was not going to get him there. If life on this island had taught him nothing else, it had taught him that. So Malcolm balanced his own pitchfork in one hand and followed the others to the barn. As he approached, he could hear David's excitement.

"What's the gun for? What kind is it? Where'd ya get it? What're ya gonna shoot?"

His father ignored the first two questions and the last, and went straight to the third.

"It's Angus MacKinnon's."

Just then George saw Minna. He stood the rifle on its stock and rested the barrel against a wall. "So, you're all working on the hay, even Curly Top." He had a smile and a pat on the head for Minna. "I think your mother's going to be needing you in the kitchen any time now." He kept his eyes on the older sister but nodded toward Barbara standing close beside him. "Why don't you two run along?"

Malcolm was outside the barn door, and his father hadn't acknowledged him yet. David was making a move toward the rifle but George caught sight of him as he turned in the direction of Don's stall.

"You can look at it but don't touch it."

David had been reaching out to take the cool barrel in both hands when his father's command made him start. He snatched his hands away and buried them in his pockets to avoid the temptation. Curiosity undampened, though, he bent his body close to the gun to examine it fully in the dim light of the stable. Malcolm watched George move deeper into the barn.

The injured horse was standing pretty much where he always stood these days, in one corner of his stall, back end to the world, head drooping into the corner. George sidled in to examine him. "Let's have a look at you, old boy."

David's attention had returned to his father now and he was hopping to catch up. "Did Mumma tell you about the accident? Don went right over the cliff! The mower is a total wreck!"

Malcolm knew David couldn't help enthusing over a major event on an island where very little excitement ever occurred, but he wished his younger brother would hold it in.

"She told me."

His father's voice was no-nonsense and muffled as he craned his head underneath the horse to look at his rear end.

"Has he been eating and making manure?"

Malcolm judged this might be as good a time as any to make his presence known. "Not much, but he's drinking though."

He put down his pitchfork and walked toward the stall. George didn't show that he'd seen his oldest son, but there was a pause and Malcolm knew the next question was directed at him, even though George's back was turned.

"Thought you'd take a shortcut to the beach, did you?"

The tone had a lazy quality and a pretend-thoughtfulness to it that Malcolm knew to be his father's version of a joke. But Malcolm had never quite grown into George's sense of humour. It was dry with a blunt edge to it, and Malcolm didn't ever know how he was supposed to take it. He could not see, for example, the humour in his nickname "Plug," or in the way his father threatened every summer to paint his children green and "let them run" as a way to save wear and tear on clothing. And, for sure, Malcolm did not see anything funny in this situation.

"Well, there's a shortcut now."

Malcolm was trying to match the mood of his father's question, but he couldn't quite make the leap from guilty perpetrator of a terrible deed to guiltless joker, insensitive to the pain he had caused. He added, "The bank must have been undercut over the winter."

George's attention appeared to be on palpitating the horse's back, looking for the sore spot, so he didn't see the twist in Malcolm's features. He may have heard it in the voice, though, because he offered, "Might have happened to anybody."

This was as close as Malcolm was going to get to forgiveness from his father, and it caught him off-guard. He didn't know how to take the words, so he did the only thing he knew to do, and that was to just keep going.

"I'll get back to the hay."

He ambled in the direction of the field, half-hoping to hear something else from his father that might confirm where he stood. All he got was "M-m-p-p-h!" as George continued to examine the horse.

Don didn't seem to be in any immediate suffering as long as he didn't try to move around. George wouldn't have to put him out of his misery tonight, at least. He would definitely have to go, but he could wait another day until an extra man could be brought over.

At suppertime, George announced he'd be bringing Angus MacKinnon over to the island the next day to help out with "some things." This cheered up the table considerably, since guests were a rare treat, indeed. David and Minna immediately began conspiring to follow Angus and their father around all day, watching what they were up to, and learning how to be grown-ups. But their father put a damper on their hopes quickly enough.

"Angus is a busy man. He'll only be here for a little while. We won't have time to be lollygaggin' with you youngsters." Then he grinned. "Maybe your mother could take you swimming."

The next day was Saturday and one of the warmest ones of the summer, so Ruth prepared for a beach day. Despite being surrounded by water and beach, the Millar children did not often swim on the island, since they would have to wait for high tide so that the rocks would be covered by water. And high tides rarely appeared in late morning or mid-afternoon, the best times for swimming.

As she set out breakfast, Ruth told the children they would be picnicking at Bayfield Beach. This was a fine stretch of sand to the south of the island and east of the wharf along the mainland shore. They would row over with George in the morning on his way to find Angus, and they would meet him as he and his friend made the return trip. No one knew what time Angus and George would be finished with their business, but the family would be able to watch at the beach for sight of the two men approaching the wharf by boat. If they began packing up then, they would easily make it in time for George to let Angus off and take them on.

On the beach, Ruth found a smooth patch of sand that had already been warmed by the morning sun. There, she spread out her blanket, sat down, and opened a new issue of *Chatelaine*. She'd received the magazine last week in the customary Sunday trade with Lena Hulbert. Only now had she found the idle time to enjoy it. Ruth imagined Lena at home doing the same thing with the issue of *Reader's Digest* she'd received in return.

Malcolm didn't feel much like playing, but he gradually loosened up as his younger brother and sisters cavorted on the beach before him. They were delighting in a warm pool of shallow water trapped by a small sandbar as the morning tide went out. This would do until the day warmed up. A little over an hour into their fun, the family stopped splashing and swimming long enough to watch two figures rowing toward the island.

There was a time when the sound of people coming through the barn door would be enough to turn Don from whatever he was doing to bob his head expectantly over his stall door. Now, it hurt too much to care. Besides, his body wouldn't do what he told it to do anymore. He used to be able to turn on a dime, to swivel his whole body around on his two back legs. He couldn't do that anymore, and food didn't interest him very much either.

Perhaps some bones in his pelvis were broken, but no one would ever know for sure. George didn't need a veterinarian to tell him what he already knew: the horse needed to be put out of its misery. Too bad. He was a good horse, and obliging, too. He had youth and strength on his side. In the last years with Jumbo, George had had to cross his fingers that the old animal was going to cope with the work he'd been asked to do. With Don, there hadn't been that concern.

George had left Angus in a clearing to finish off the digging while he went back to the barn for the horse. The clearing was too far away from the house and the rest of the farm to be used for anything practical, except to bury dead animals. Jumbo had been laid to rest here, and Don would be, too.

Don still had his head to the wall, but he turned it in a weak greeting to his master.

"Let's take a walk, old fellow."

George was in the habit of saying "old fellow" after so many years with Jumbo, even though this horse was young. Don's head was heavy as George slipped on his halter and grasped it with one hand. He gently tugged: once, twice. On the third tug the horse began making tentative steps and slowly turned his body around to point himself in the direction of his stall door.

It is often said an animal knows when its time is nigh and will accept it with a kind of stoicism that leaves its handlers humbled. This was Don's attitude today. He offered no resistance when George coaxed him down the gentle slope into the burying hole, even though this was the hardest part for his ailing back end. When Angus leveled his rifle at a point between the beast's eyes, Don stared dumbly ahead, blinking slowly, making no sound and no movement to get away. It was over before the thunder-clap of the shot left the air. Don slumped into the fresh clay, lifeless and free from pain without ever making a single protest.

Before the two men started tossing clay back into the hole, George did one more thing. He knelt down, and from Don's lifeless head, slipped the leather halter. There was nothing to be gained by burying a perfectly good piece of harness that would cost money to replace. The price of another horse was going to be enough.

Clods of iron-red earth pattered onto Don's body as the two men began to shovel. George was trying to keep his gaze upward when he spotted a bottle propped against a tree trunk in the shade. Angus must have brought it over, concealed in his overalls that very morning. The men would no doubt be thirsty after their work.

On Bayfield Beach, Ruth and the children were eating their picnic lunch when the sound of Don's death split the silence. It was a quiet day on the harbour and the water was smooth, so there was little to muffle the noise from the rifle. It seemed to fly across the water like a bullet itself, splitting the air and vibrating overhead. Although neither Malcolm nor Ruth had ever heard a gunshot, they both immediately recognized the sound. Malcolm had been about to take a bite from his sandwich, but the sound of the shot caught him before he'd even settled his teeth all the way through.

He almost took the sandwich out of his mouth with just the tooth marks to mar it, but he realized that wouldn't be practical. So he closed his jaw and kept on eating. The heavy, salty flavour of the ham almost made him sick. The younger ones began to buzz. "What was that? It sounded like it came from the island." A moment of uncertain silence gripped the small group on the beach, and Ruth felt compelled to break it before someone started putting clues together out loud.

"Finish up your lunches, now. There won't be much more time for play before we have to start heading back to the wharf."

"Mumma, was that a gunshot?" David was too precocious sometimes. "Did it come from over-home?"

She didn't look at either of her sons, but began packing up the remnants of lunch. "You and Malcolm should get busy at that sandcastle if you're going to get it finished before we have to leave."

She pointed to the smooth wet beach, larger by a few feet now than it had been when they'd arrived. "The tide's out far enough now for a nice big one."

Ruth shaded her eyes with one hand and looked toward the island. From her vantage point on the beach, she could see a long sandbar looming up in the water about a quarter-mile out. This deposit, left by tides, currents, and movement of winter ice, snaked nearly a half-mile from the landing end of Pomquet Island and curled into the bay in this direction. She knew that eventually she would see the faraway forms of George and Angus emerging from behind it and rowing toward Bayfield wharf.

Minna was actually the first to spot the men about an hour and a half after the beach picnic was put away.

"There's Daddy and Angus!" she called from where she and Barbara were squatting over a collection of seashells and smooth stones, which they were going to use to decorate the sandcastle.

Ruth got up from her blanket where she'd been absorbed in her reading. "Let's get ready to meet them."

The walk from the beach to the wharf took about twenty minutes, with the children stopping every so often to re-gather tumbling towels and blankets, or to examine interesting shells and stones. When the picnic group reached the wharf, George and Angus had already been there for a while. They were passing the time by shooting the breeze with a few fishermen still organizing their gear after bringing in their early-morning catches. Angus was holding the rifle in one hand. It rested casually along his leg as he talked. The other hand was wrapped around the long handle of his shovel. He leaned on it as he spoke.

A slow smile warmed his weather-grizzled face as the children approached. "Did you have a good swim then, dears?" He was looking at Minna and Barbara, who still carried the shells and stones that had been meant for the castle. "And what've ya got there?"

After briefly teasing the girls, Angus turned his attention to the boys. David had his eye on the gun, and Malcolm was looking at the shovel. There was fresh dirt on it.

David looked from the gun barrel to Angus's face and back again. He couldn't hold it in. "Did you fire that shot?"

Ruth stopped him there. "That's enough, David. Don't interrupt when the adults are talking."

The older man caught on quickly. "You boys look like yus were doin' some buildin'."

Angus was eyeing the sand still plastered to their shins and knees. Embarrassed, the two began to brush the dirt away.

He turned toward Ruth, who by now had covered her bathing suit with a summer shift. "And how are you, Missus Millar? You had a nice outing with the young ones, did you?"

Angus was taller and lankier than George. He wore sagging denim overalls and a peaked cap that showed its utility in the sweat and salt stains that ringed its crown.

"Yes, thank you, Angus, I did."

Ruth knew Angus and George had been friends for a long time, gladly helping each other whenever help was required. Ruth thought Angus a fine enough person, but she didn't mind that he lived far enough away so as to not be a constant influence on the children.

George squatted at the edge of the wharf, making the rowboat ready for its next load of passengers. The effort forced his words a bit. "Maybe you'll come over some day soon and have a meal with us."

Once everyone was settled in—George with two oars, David and Malcolm at the bow and stern with an oar each—the Millar family said their good-byes and pushed off toward home.

Angus was watching them go, still with the shovel propped in one hand and the rifle in the other: "P'raps on a Sunday while it's still fine I'll bring the missus over after church."

It was only mid-afternoon by the time they got home. Minna and Barbara followed their mother into the house to help with the chores that hadn't been done yet today. Meanwhile, George and the boys headed for the barn to pick up their forks and continue stacking the rest of the hay.

In a stab at courage, Malcolm decided he might as well ask his father the question that had been on his mind the entire way across the bay. "How are we going to get the hay in without Don to pull the drag?"

"Frank Randall's going to loan us his horse after he finishes haying."

David ran ahead and into the barn. Moments later he came back out scratching his head and looking toward the pasture where the two milk cows, noses in the grass, took no notice.

"Where's Don?"

George took a few strides to answer because he wanted to be within easy speaking distance of both sons. "We had to put him down."

"You and Angus? Why?"

David's second question was close to a whine, and Malcolm could see tears welling in his little brother's eyes. He knew his father could see them, too.

"He was too badly hurt."

Malcolm was trying not to show that his own eyes were misting, so he stared at his feet. That was a bad idea because it made his nose run. So, he turned around to squint at the cows, the hay—anything not to look at his father and brother.

"Just because he couldn't pull anything anymore doesn't mean you had to shoot him!" protested the younger boy.

Malcolm kept his mouth shut, but he was starting to pace now, feeling the discomfort of his part in Don's demise. David could say nothing more, only wipe his eyes with the backs of his hands.

George gave both boys a minute to compose themselves, and then—with some force—admonished, "You might as well get used to this now. If you do any amount of farming at all, you'll soon realize that animals die. You can't go pining away after every one of them."

He strode into the barn, picked up his fork, and headed for the hayfield. Reluctantly, Malcolm and David followed.

George might have been able to sell Don to a fox rancher for meat. A big animal like that probably would have brought a decent sum. But no prospective buyers were brought to the island to have a look at him. Angus had brought over an extra shovel instead.

A few days later, Malcolm was carrying water from the well to the house when his eye caught something glinting in the sunlight on the beach below. He didn't remember seeing it when Don was led this way on the day of the accident. Later, when he got a break from his chores, Malcolm went to investigate. The clear bottle was already partly buried in the coarse sand, but the colours were still bright on the label, and it read clearly enough: "Old Rye Whiskey. Joseph E. Seagram."

[The interim lightkeepers] had a dog named Victor and a large male cat called Benghazi. Minna and I were quite shocked the first time we visited to find that Benghazi was being fed from a saucer of Grandmother Mitchell's heirloom dishes. —Barbara Millar

The Mainland Years

CHAPTER NINE

Ruth couldn't do it herself. Or, she wasn't going to be allowed to do it herself, that's what it amounted to. She was going to have to move her four youngest children to the mainland and wait out her husband's World War II service away from their island. That was how they'd grown to think of it by now: *their* island. For sixteen years they'd coaxed crops from its scrubby soil, raised generations of livestock, brought up children, and nested into the moods and vagaries of the weather and the sea.

The thought of someone else caring for their place rankled Ruth. She was as capable as any man of keeping the flame burning in the light tower. There certainly were precedents—many lights owed their continuation to the widows of the men who'd been hired to keep them. Ruth could row a boat, hitch a horse, or milk a cow as well as the next person.

To be fair, though, there was an added element of hardship for a woman biding her time on an island with a farm, four children, and a light—even with Malcolm nearly a full-grown man. Managing travel to and from the mainland would be that much more difficult without George there. None of them knew the ice and the tides the way he did. So, whether by government fiat or by George's design (no one would ever know for sure), Jack Henderson was awarded the temporary job.

George came home one December day in 1940 to give Ruth the news. She was kneading bread dough at the dry sink in the dining room. The woodstove had already been moved to this room for the winter, so that it was now both kitchen and eating area.

"Well, there you have it: I'm not a person, just a wife. Wives don't keep lights." She kept on kneading.

George did a double take behind Ruth's back as he picked up the daily paper on his way past the dining table. *Where did that come from? Nellie McClung, likely, via Lena Hulbert's* Chatelaine. Even after all those warnings he'd given her. "Now, little woman, you're not going to manage this island by yourself," he would say late at night after the children had gone to bed. "It'll still be here when the war's over." But George knew that sometimes Ruth just got an idea in her head and ran with it. Well, he guessed, she'd have to get used to a new idea.

No sense rehashing all those conversations now, though. George expelled his reply with a soft grunt as he sank into the rocking chair next to the range. "Maybe that's it."

His view was of Ruth's back across the room and the intermittent ripples through the hem of her dress as she pressed hands and shoulders into her task. George opened his mouth to say something else, then thought better of it. He knew by each thump of Ruth's fists into the bread dough and the tautness in her voice that it was best not to poke that nest. Without another word he opened the *Morning Chronicle*, stretched his arms, shook the paper stiff, and began to read the war news: "Rumania Newest Member of Axis"; "Shipping Crisis Deepens." Truth be told, he was glad his wife and children were going to wait out the war safe on the mainland.

In the silence between them, Ruth considered the situation. Not only was she going to have to give up her husband for a few years—that, she had been resigned to from the beginning—but she was going to have to give up her home, too. This from the same government that was likely going to be asking for her oldest son if the war went on through 1943. And if the headlines could be looked to as a guide, it probably would go on. She worked the bread mixture some more, but said nothing. When Ruth had shaped the puffy dough, rubbed it shiny with warm lard, and dropped it into pans for baking, George picked up the conversation again.

"Minnie Stewart and the young fellow might be glad to have someone around for the winter. I'll look into it next time I'm over to the mainland."

"Mmm-hmm."

Ruth opened the oven door and slid in four pans of dough. It wasn't the first time she'd made do in temporary quarters, but her memories of previous winters on the mainland—waiting to give birth to Minna, then David and, lastly, Barbara—weren't calling her back to shore. From a half-kneel in front of the stove, she heaved the oven door shut, then straightened stiffly. That wasn't as easy as it used to be. With one hand, she rubbed the small of her back as she stood quietly regarding the door she'd just closed.

But Ruth was a Presbyterian, raised to be grateful for what she had. *No sense bucking what you can't change.* It was best to be practical and turn to planning the move. Massaging the stiffness from her hands, Ruth made a half-turn to face her husband, who was still behind the newspaper. A militia man, he was expecting to be called up any day now.

"Perhaps your orders won't come 'til summer so we can all settle in."

She moved to the dry sink and began tidying up. She didn't notice George lowering the newspaper behind her as she carried the floured mixing tub into the summer kitchen for washing.

"Henderson starts in April, so we can go in January after the light closes down."

George raised the paper again. That was easier than he'd thought, so he continued: "We'll be able to walk the animals on the ice by then. I'll see if the Chisholms or the Suttons want them."

Ruth was looking for positives now. One thing she could be glad of was her experience with moving. She had by now honed her ability to judge what the family would need and what could stay behind.

Dad was the type of person who accepted life for what it was and made the best of any situation. When we worked together, he would always say, "When you are doing anything, give it your best shot." —David Millar

There did always seem to be someone on the mainland willing to provide accommodations—that was something to be thankful for. No use complaining, then. Ruth would do what her parents had done, and what George was doing, too: she would make the best of the situation at hand and never mind griping over what she couldn't control.

It had been little more than a year earlier that George had come into this very room to bring Ruth the other news. "Well, they're at it," was all he said as he took a seat by the radio in the dining room and began working the dials.

Ruth had known, in the way that she always knew, exactly what her husband meant. War had been declared on Germany, and the Battle of the Atlantic had begun.

From that moment forward, Ruth had been playing out scenarios in her mind, trying to figure out how she would tend the light and marshal her four youngest children to do the chores in George's absence. Not long after George had given her this news, the National

Resources Mobilization Act took effect, and George knew he would play some part in training conscripts the government was enlisting for home defence, one of the primary tasks of the Non-Permanent Active Militia (NPAM).

In January of 1941, after George extinguished the last light for the winter, the Millar household relocated temporarily to the mainland home of Minnie Stewart and her son, John B. As soon as they could, George and Ruth began to look for long-term accommodations, but they were momentarily sidetracked by what happened next.

In their sheltered life on the island, the children had not been exposed to the usual childhood illnesses. Now on the mainland, they had some catching up to do. First, it was Minna and David. They caught whooping cough almost as soon as they started back at school in Bayfield. The family's introduction to life in the Stewart household was highlighted by Ruth's nighttime trips between the son and the daughter. One would cough until he threw up, the other, until her nose bled. But that wasn't the worst of it.

Seventeen-year-old Rosa had only recently been rushed to the tiny community of Farmington to help fill a wartime teacher shortage. Having just finished grade twelve by correspondence from her grandparents' home in Pugwash, she met the school inspector's new and less rigorous criteria. This she had achieved despite her grandfather's frequent floor-pacing protests: "Educatin' women! No good will ever come from educatin' women!" In this case, it began to look as if he may have been right. Rosa had barely settled into her billeted accommodations when she began coughing and losing weight.

The lady of the house offered her own armchair prognosis on a daily basis. "You'll fill an early grave, my dear." It did not seem to occur to the landlady that a bit more heat might prevent this forecast from coming to pass.

This judgment she would issue as she rocked back and forth in her chair by the kitchen stove, teacup and saucer balanced on her ample midsection. "I never saw nobody that coughed so much and got so thin that didn't have consumption."

Her head would wag from side to side as she spoke, and Rosa would have no choice but to listen as she shivered at the kitchen table while preparing her lessons for the next day.

"Mark my words, girl. You'll fill an early grave."

Soon all twelve pupils, from beginners through grade eight, began coughing and whooping. Thus, Rosa's condition was diagnosed. Not only did she have whooping cough, but she had brought it to the entire community. There was nothing else to do but close down the school until everyone recovered. Rosa was sent back to her mother's care in Bayfield.

About the time Rosa was finally ready to go back to work, she received a letter from the school inspector who had issued her teacher's permit for Farmington. Enclosed with his note was one on behalf of the community, declaring good riddance to the teacher accused of bringing whooping cough to the children. Furthermore, the writers attested, they did not want Rosa back. The inspector, however, felt differently. He vowed that if Farmington did not accept Rosa, the community would not get a teacher at all. It was to this less-than-ideal welcome that she returned to finish the school term. At least her new billet would be more comfortable and slightly more cheerful than the last. Rosa's willingness to go back into the jaws of the lion so impressed the inspector that he encouraged her to go on to normal school (later known as teachers' college). With this less-than-auspicious beginning, her career was launched.

By this time, Ruth might have been excused for wishing none of them had ever left the island. She and George were still trying to find a long-term home, so there was really no time to feel sorry for herself or her children. But how many homes were there in this small community—occupied or unoccupied—that could take in a family of six, just like that? It wasn't until the spring that the Millars finally found a more permanent home with Connor Boyle, a bachelor farmer who had a large house and a view of the school just across the field. This good news was important, because the trials of mainland life were only beginning, and illness would not let go its hold just yet.

Thelma had been able to escape the whooping cough, having left home a few weeks before the family moved from Pomquet Island. But the Aberdeen Hospital School of Nursing was an unsparing introduction to adulthood. The demands were rigorous and the discipline strict, although these aspects in themselves were not alien to nineteen-year-old Thelma. It was probably the strangeness of it all that did her in.

Having never before had occasion to be homesick, she did not even have a name for the feelings of malaise that overcame her soon after she arrived in New Glasgow. But when the house mother found her crying alone one morning in the small room she shared with three other students, a name for Thelma's complaint came to mind quickly enough: red measles. A childhood illness in an adult body was no small matter. The course of the disease would be longer, and Thelma much sicker, than if she were a child with the same complaint.

Even after recovery, Thelma did not thrive in her new setting. Luckily, the nursing school superiors were not heartless people, and they took note of the young student's difficulty. Having shrunk to less than one hundred pounds with no apparent weight gain in sight, she was judged unfit to continue with her curriculum until she spent some time at home. Along with the leave from school, Thelma was instructed to think about whether she really wanted to be a nurse after all. Like Rosa, though, Thelma would not declare defeat: as soon as she was strong enough, she returned to school. In the coming years, mumps and German measles would be added to her resumé of illnesses contracted before graduation in 1944.

Ironically, it would be another communicable disease that would give Thelma the freedom to set an early career path. Because she had been exposed to tuberculosis during Sunday visits to the Hulberts' house as a child, she was immune to the disease. This helped her decide to take up a nursing position at the Kentville Sanatorium, where she remained for several years nursing TB patients.

If the Millar resolve served the family well that first winter on the mainland, it was not enough to save the cat. When the Millars were on the island, Polly had managed quite comfortably on barn mice, birds, and a daily squirt of milk that George would aim into an old sardine can while he was milking the cows.

But Polly didn't want to move to the mainland, even though all of her barn companions had left, and along with them, her daily ration of milk. With the Hendersons not yet moved in and no continuing food source, it was not long before the mice vacated, too. To make conditions still worse, the birds that were easiest to catch, like sparrows and robins, began looking farther afield once the chickens and their daily feedings vanished.

Relocating Polly became a personal challenge for Malcolm: three times he tried and three times he failed to bring Polly to the Millars' new home. The first time, he walked with John B. over the ice to the island. He put the cat under his warm coat until he reached the house on the mainland and hoped she would stay where she could readily find food and warmth. But Polly preferred the surroundings she knew best and disappeared soon after. Twice more, Malcolm searched her out and put her in a burlap bag so that she couldn't see where she was going. But Polly's internal compass proved stronger than all of her master's efforts. The last time he went to find her, Malcolm again found Polly in the barn. But this time, she was curled up in a leftover pile of musty straw, frozen in eternal sleep.

In January of 1942, George's orders finally came. Corporal Millar was to report to No. 61 NPAM Training Centre, just outside New Glasgow on an old industrial site, unofficially known as Parkdale Camp. He would be a drill instructor, helping to bring young men through basic training. At the end of their training, these recruits could volunteer for overseas duty in any branch of military service, or they could continue as conscripts to be called up for home defence if needed.

Those who chose to stay at home were reviled by many as "zombies" and laggards. How could they be entrusted with Canada's home defence while the cream of the country's fighting men—those with the vigour to volunteer—were marching into the fire overseas? George couldn't help but agree with the critics in the beginning, but, having met the enemy face-to-face himself, he could understand a man's reluctance to rush an encounter. Still, it stumped him how a healthy young man could hang back from volunteering in a time of war. What kind of person would force his country force him into service? Duty was duty, after all, and every young man had a duty to his country.

As time went on, though, George saw in the conscripts many qualities he'd seen in himself and his fighting companions two-and-a-half decades earlier. True, some wished they could be anywhere else but Parkdale. Others, though, resolutely accepted their fate and took to their training with purpose. Having been on the front lines, George knew something that the conscripts' critics did not: in the heat of battle, any man—forced recruit or not—could surprise you with the heights of his courage or the depths of his cowardice. No matter what their circumstances, he would give these men his best.

Looking ahead to 1943, George knew his oldest son wouldn't be a zombie. There had not been much discussion about it, but discussion wasn't necessary. George had raised his children to know their duty, and it was clear where Malcolm's obligation would lie if the war was still raging past his eighteenth birthday. George knew, too, that Thelma would be signing up for the medical corps if the fighting was still on when she graduated from nursing school. Service was bred into George and Ruth Millar's children; they didn't need to be told.

Knowing well George's instinct for authority, it would come as no surprise to his children that their father would soon become acting orderly sergeant at Parkdale, after daily route marches with recruits became impossible due to a bone spur in his heel. Nor would it surprise his children that little more than a year after his enlistment, George would be recommended for promotion to warrant officer. Even though the promotion never came, George seemed comfortable in the military, and he was well-regarded by his superiors.

Back in Bayfield, Ruth was having to make her own painful adjustments. She would never say she was not grateful for the roof over her head. Nor was it easy to dismiss the convenience of the children's short walk to school. Still, life was not entirely smooth with a bachelor whose main priorities had always been outside the home. The one blessing was that, if Connor wasn't in the barn or the chicken coop, he was probably visiting his lady friend a few miles away. Long-time bachelor that he was, Connor was content to keep only one bedroom for himself and let the Millars use the rest of the house. He didn't need very much to make his life finer than it had been previously. Good food and a bit of housekeeping were all he required in return. But somewhere in the back of her mind, Ruth knew the arrangement couldn't be that simple.

The kicker came one early April evening. Connor was seated alone at the kitchen table finishing a late plate of corned beef and cabbage when he brought it up. Ruth was at the counter setting out a batch of biscuits to cool, getting the jump on the next day's meals.

"Yer not usin' the front parlour fer anything are ya, Mrs. Millar?" came the question through a mouth full of bread sopped in the supper juice remaining on Connor's plate.

Ruth thought for a moment. It would be nice to have a room where she could entertain her church group and quilting friends, but no one used the large dining room either. Maybe Connor would consent to her putting that room into shape in return for keeping the other to himself. Having regular visitors would be one luxury of mainland life.

"I'm thinkin' I'd like ta use it fer a few months," he added, words a little clearer this time, having swallowed his bread.

Ruth couldn't really object to the owner of the house making use of his own parlour—coal stove and all—perhaps to store some things or to take in a friend.

"No, Connor, we're not really using it at all, except when David and Barbara play in there."

"Good then! I'm bringin' in some brooder chicks. They'll pra'bly be here tamorra. Gonna keep 'em warm in there with the base burner 'til they git their feathers."

This was a good time for Ruth to bring her maxim into play: "If you can't say anything good about something, don't say anything at all." Connor was the landlord after all, and she wasn't going to find another home for herself and four children in a hurry. She and George had already exhausted every option before settling on this place.

"Well, we can't have them getting into the rest of the house!" was all she could think of to say before leaving the kitchen and picking up her knitting on the way out.

"Oh, no, ma'am!" Connor was saying to her back while making one more pass with his bread around the rim of his dinner plate. "Be too cold for 'em."

True to his word, early the next morning Connor—like many of his contemporaries routinely did—began setting up the unused room for his day-old chicks. At first it wasn't so bad—as long as guests were made aware that the constant scratching and peeping sounds, seemingly from rats inside the walls, were just the chicks scurrying around on the floor of the parlour. But after a week or so, the smell of the chicks and all that went with them threatened to overpower anyone who opened the door to their brooding room. How could one host meetings or quilting with that going on? It wouldn't do for her lady friends to think she was living in squalor. Ruth was almost apoplectic, but there was really no one to tell. Ruth was a quiet sort most of the time anyway, so she did not go looking for people whose ears she could bend.

It was a warm July morning when Connor began removing the chicks from their room and depositing them in the barnyard. Ruth happened to be in the kitchen and stood by, dishtowel in hand, watching the transfer. Connor would wade into the room, swooping after the nearly grown chicks. He would gather a few at a time and remove them in a large wire cage while they murmured with anxiety inside. A draft of warm, chick-laden air caught Ruth and almost bowled her over. She could see sunlight streaking across a fine, white dust that seemed to cover every surface in the room. Only the strong of heart would want that cleaning job, and Ruth wasn't sure she was one of them.

"Connor, you'll be wanting to open the windows in there so the room can air out," she advised, voice muffled by the towel she was holding against her nose. She turned back to her work at the kitchen counter. Connor shooed another chick into the cage and latched the wire door.

"Don't worry yerself, Mrs. Millar. I'll look after it all. That'll be my room now."

"Fine with me."

Connor might not have heard Ruth, because she had her back to him and she was wiping down the countertop with extra vigour.

The next spring, whether through heightened sensitivity to Ruth's distaste for living with newly hatched chicks or for a change of scenery, Connor set up his brooder in an unused room above the kitchen. This was an improvement because the smell did not waft through the rest of the house. Still, the scratching and peeping heard through the ceiling could be a distraction at times. Mercifully, the year after that, Connor built a brooder house in the yard, where he kept his chicks from that time forward.

No one could ignore that the war years were a disruptive time for the whole family. Ruth would sometimes catch herself looking off in the direction of Pomquet Island when she was out and about in the community. She would find herself picturing the kitchen, or her garden, or the parlour with the coal stove lit in the winter. But then she would have to look away and remind herself there was no use being homesick. She would have to trust that her island was being properly cared for by the Hendersons.

Ruth made some trips across the bay after that first winter, but not many. Childless themselves, the Hendersons enjoyed the company of the Millar children on infrequent visits. But Ruth pretty much stayed away—it was better that way. After all, this was a time of uncertainty for everyone. At least Ruth didn't have anyone overseas to worry about—not yet anyway. Besides, everyone in the Millar family—whether living with her or elsewhere—had four walls around them, clean clothes to wear, and enough to eat. Many people "over there" in Europe couldn't say the same. Disruption was the price exacted by duty in a time of war and, just like George, Ruth was willing to pay it.

For the children, living on the mainland did not seem difficult at all—just the opposite, in fact. For the first time in her life, Barbara had playmates within walking distance, and her schooling began exactly the way it did for the other children in Bayfield: with a short walk. Minna, David, and Malcolm delighted in being able to stay after school to participate in games and practices for concerts, and all enjoyed the benefits of being able to attend school year-round.

It did not take the Millar children long to become fully involved in school life. That first winter on the mainland, Minna was given a Christmas poem to recite at the concert, and all of the children helped decorate for the big event. For Minna, there was even a new blue dress—her first long dress—made by her mother on the treadle sewing machine she'd insisted on bringing with her from the island.

John Colin [Henderson] and his wife Mary had no children of their own but liked children very much, so Minna and I would visit occasionally in the summer, and David often went to stay for a few days. John Colin was a kind man and, when they were available, he would buy us chocolate bars, which were a real treat during the war. They tasted like lard and sawdust but we thought they were good.
—Barbara Millar

It was not a sure thing that George would be able to spend every Christmas Day in Bayfield, but he would usually be granted some leave during the holiday season. When he did come home there was great excitement around his visits and he would always bring books, the customary gift for each child.

Still, the observance of Christmas would not be as sheltered and snug as it had been on the island. Christmas morning no longer came alive with the excited voices of all six children. Living more than one hundred miles westward along the coast, Rosa would sometimes be kept away by weather, and, as a nurse-in-training, Thelma would often have to fill the vacation gap left by others more senior. Nevertheless, family celebrations were memorable enough. There would be a turkey or a chicken for dinner, as many sweets as wartime rationing would allow and, possibly, attendance at the Christmas worship in Afton.

Times were changing, and George was changing, too. For one thing, there was no longer a farm to manage, and with two children living independently and a third almost ready to go, there was not as much family managing to do either. The distance seemed to have become a benefit somehow: George was becoming more relaxed as a parent. But the changes in their father were less obvious to most of the children than they were to Thelma the day she attended her first dance at Parkdale Camp in the summer of 1943.

Thelma's first sight of her father was across the empty parade square, and she felt her stomach muscles harden. Only at that moment did she realize how familiar the feeling was, and only at that moment did she realize the cause.

It was their first visit since George had started his service at Parkdale more than a year before. Thelma fussed with her purse and sweater in the back seat of the black VIP car, and the young conscript her father had sent to fetch her seemed to pick up on her tension. Private McQuaid put on an extra show of efficiency for his former drill instructor as he slid crisply from behind the steering wheel and, with a flourish, stepped sideways, pulled open the rear door, and offered a gloved hand to Thelma as she climbed into the sunlight.

Her father was quickly shortening the distance between them. Either George had been watching for the car, or it was just coincidence that the moment she arrived, he had been exiting, in full uniform, from the Commanding Officer's building well after his day's work should have ended. The sound of his boots on the parade square pavement accented the three gold chevrons on his khaki sleeves as his arms moved in a not-quite-march. The low evening sunlight burnished a single line of brass buttons that held together his belted jacket. Ribbons on his chest signifying two service medals from the previous war were the only other splash of colour against the olive drab. There was no need for Thelma to meet her father halfway, and she couldn't have anyway. She was pinned to the spot.

Thelma stood at the hump of the car's rear fender with purse in hand and sweater draped over her arm. She had thought herself well turned out, too, as she had admired her new clothes in the mirror at the student nurses' residence. She would have preferred her hair cut short rather than having it rolled and tucked about her already-round face; she would have liked to replace the wire glasses that cut into her cheeks every time she smiled; and she would have liked to trade in her lisles for a pair of nylon stockings. The war had taken away her chances at any of these, but Thelma was still happy with her new outfit. She'd scrimped enough money to buy new shoes and a dress from her meagre pay and the extra two-dollar bills her mother sent along sporadically. There were mixed feelings, though, about trying them out at this Saturday night party on an army base where her own father would be among the chaperones.

Dances at Parkdale Camp had become popular among the locals, but Thelma had heard enough about the base to know why she was there. It was difficult to find unattached young women willing to partner with the recruits who'd been branded zombies. It did not surprise Thelma that her father would encourage her to attend a dance like this. She knew him to be practical, but she also knew him to have a sense of fun, even if it was too often buried under a sense of necessity. Anyway, she imagined he was counting on his oldest daughter's encounters being too brief to form lasting attachments.

When George had come close enough for Thelma to make out the detail on his cap, she braced for their first communication. It might be a remark about how pale or thin she looked after having only recently recovered from the German measles. But she could already see the corners of his mouth turned up under his stiff moustache, and there was a glint of teeth in the smile. As he came almost close enough to touch, Thelma was taken aback by the softness in her father's eyes.

"Are you ready for a dance?"

George grinned at his daughter. This friendly attitude was not completely unfamiliar. After all, from an early age it was she who had been designated his second-in-command over her younger brothers and sisters. Still, easiness of manner was not commonplace between George and his children.

"I guess so…" She sounded tentative, and she knew her father didn't like indecision. "I've been practising with the girls at the school."

That was a little better.

Thelma was like her mother in shape, but her once-blonde hair had long ago gone dark, nearly as dark as her father's. It was thick, too, almost too thick to manage. Where Ruth's features were fine and light, Thelma's were more like George's: a short, broad nose, low forehead and a definite brow. The genes that gave her father a fleshy face made Thelma's round and chubby, regardless of her body weight. Her blue eyes favoured her mother's, however, and she was an attractive dance partner for any young recruit.

"Well, let's see who's going to fight over you, then."

Thelma wasn't sure if her father had just paid her a compliment, so she said nothing. George offered his elbow and she took it, although this, too, was something entirely unaccustomed. As they walked toward the dance hall, Private McQuaid slid into the VIP car and drove away.

It could not be said that George became softer during his time away from home, but it might be said that he became more tolerant of softness in others. Perhaps it came from recognizing his own fallibility, demonstrated by the aches and pains of age. Maybe it had something to do with a parent seeing his children as adults for the first time, as he did when he saw Thelma dressed up for the Parkdale dances, Rosa with a well-intentioned suitor, or Malcolm in uniform. Or perhaps it had something to do with training young men to go off into battle, knowing that not all of them would return. Against all of this, a small weakness here or there might be excusable after all.

If the war had changed George, it changed Ruth as well. She could not remain the same when her circumstances had altered so much. No longer were things as ordered as they had been on the island, nor were they as austere. Modern conveniences were now close at hand, the children had friends to play with outside of school, and Ruth was independent from her husband for the most part. The family car—previously kept at the wharf and used infrequently—was now at her disposal, as long as she did not drive farther than the wartime gasoline ration allowed. With the children attending school year-round, Ruth found the supervision of their study much less demanding than it had been on the island. She now had time for other pursuits.

These pursuits included putting the car to good use. The goodwill of the Millars' mainland neighbours had more than once helped them out of difficult situations, and full-time access to an automobile presented an opportunity to return the kindness. Thus, Ruth and the car became Bayfield's informal taxi service, whether she wanted the job or not. Frequently, she was called upon to drive people to medical and business appointments and once even rushed a badly burned boy to the hospital in Antigonish. As time went by, requests for her services became more frequent, and Ruth sometimes felt the heaviness of her new responsibility. Still, her role was all part of an existence so completely alien to the lightkeeping life that Ruth had long since

Life on the mainland was a real treat because now we could develop friendships with the other children of the community. We now could take part in nighttime activities, skating and coasting in the winter and swimming in the summer. We were able to take part in the Christmas concert and attend National Film Board movies at night.
—David Millar

learned to let the tide of events take her where it willed. That did not stop her, though, from wishing the interminable war would come to an end—before her eldest son had to join the fight.

By July of 1943, Malcolm had a decision to make. Enlistment was expected of him, so his decision was not whether he would volunteer for overseas service, but with which branch. As a child, Malcolm had read his Dave Dawson books with relish, and stories of Billy Bishop also rang in his head for years. In 1943, Buzz Beurling, the decorated WWII flying ace from Verdun, Quebec, was the hero of the skies. He had already shot down more enemy planes than Malcolm had fingers and toes on which to count them, and his daring exploits captured Malcolm's imagination.

As a result, Malcolm decided he would be a flying ace, too. But at his physical examination, he was judged colour blind. This meant he could not be a pilot, but the disappointment did not kill his desire to work with airplanes, so he chose to be a mechanic instead. It was a momentous occasion for both Ruth and George to see their son leave home, then to see him return at Christmas dressed—but for the cap and stripes—in the same khakis as his father.

By late 1944, matters closer to home were calling for Ruth's attention. Connor was planning to wed the woman he had been courting. Ruth and her remaining three children would have to find yet another place to live. But the search was not quite as difficult this time. Just down the Wharf Road, near the beach and almost within hailing distance of the breakwater, Ella Mae Grant's former home sat unoccupied. It was surrounded by apple trees, a woodlot, and as many berries as a person could pick.

Ruth could keep Pomquet Island in sight now whenever she wished. Walking down the tree-lined road and seeing the island was like finding light at the end of a tunnel. Surely, the war would be over soon. Even though the household was becoming progressively easier to manage with Minna now fifteen, David thirteen, and Barbara nine, Ruth could not rest until she, her husband, and her children were back where they belonged.

By the spring of 1945, Ruth, Minna, David, and Barbara were well settled into their new home. One warm, sunny day in early May, the nearby neighbours, who were relatives of the owner, had come by to cut firewood for their winter supply. By way of entertainment, they had pulled their car up close to the work area and turned the radio on. David was near the car helping with the stacking when he heard the first news bulletin:

"We interrupt this program to bring you an unconfirmed report that Germany has surrendered!"

David dropped the wood he was carrying and ran into the house, not bothering to shut the screen door behind him. The racket jarred Ruth's attention from the dress she was sewing at the treadle machine. It hadn't been easy keeping up George's level of discipline with the children, but Ruth had done her best. By now, though, she was tiring of exaggerating her reactions to her children's indiscretions. She knit her brows and inhaled, ready to order her son to close the door properly. But her expression dissolved as quickly as it had appeared when she began to make sense of her son's words.

"Turn on the radio! Quick! Germany surrendered!"

The intended scolding forgotten, Ruth left her sewing where it sat on the machine and followed David into the dining room. On a table near the window was the family radio, which had been shipped from the island with care. By the time Ruth made it into the room, David had already turned on the power and the indicator dial was illuminated. It took a few moments for the instrument to warm up and for a faraway voice to be heard.

"...now that the original report is false. We have no reports to confirm that Germany has surrendered. Stay tuned and we will bring you any breaking news as soon as we have it."

It was an extravagant thing to do, but Ruth did not need persuading when David suggested that they keep the radio turned on all day. By the time the children had gone off to bed at eight o'clock, there was still no official news of surrender. Ruth sat by the radio and continued darning socks by the light of an oil lamp. Then, just after

9:30, the announcement came: "Germany has surrendered unconditionally."

Ruth's darning fell to her lap and she allowed her shoulders to sag. For only the second time in her life did she realize how much she had been holding in, and for how long. At last it was over. Now they could all go home.

Even after two years of retirement, I find it hard to realize that I can make plans regarding going some place without adding the phrase used so often in thirty-five years, "wind and weather permitting."
—George Millar

Time of Extinguishing

CHAPTER TEN

*O*f course Ruth knew that the way you dress things up in your imagination is not always the way they turn out in real life. She prided herself on being practical but, somehow, readjusting to the lightkeeping life did not come as easily as it did when she had played it out in her mind.

In fact, she and the children had grown quite fond of their new home on the Wharf Road, and they were not anxious to leave it. They had grown accustomed to the conveniences of mainland life. When George returned to Bayfield just before Christmas in 1945, he and

Ruth decided to stay in the house for the winter, to allow the children to finish another year of school on the mainland. Besides, the Hendersons would need time to find a new situation, and George would need to get a start on gathering livestock to take back to the island.

The following spring was not a happy one for Minna, now seventeen. Old enough to work at part-time jobs and sociable enough to enjoy mixing with other teenagers, she was not anxious for the isolation a move to Pomquet Island would bring. Her parents soon understood that she would be happier living with the newly wed Rosa in Pugwash. There, she finished grade twelve by correspondence and kept house while Rosa taught school. That left David and Barbara on the island with their parents since Malcolm had not yet been discharged from the RCAF. His mechanic's skills were needed in England, where the Royal Air Force was just winding down its massive war effort.

By now, David was old enough to row himself and his sister to and from the mainland so they could attend the small green schoolhouse. The men at the wharf soon dubbed them "Captain" and "First Mate." At fifteen, David was old enough that, when he was not in school, he could be a substantial help to his father with the boats, the fishing, and the farming. An eleven-year-old girl did not have as many choices of occupation, though, and even the busy fishermen at Bayfield wharf could see that Barbara was lonely.

> *"You lived on an island? How romantic!"*
>
> *What makes one think that way?*
>
> *I lived on one, it wasn't so—*
>
> *My friends lived 'cross the bay.*
>
> *—Minna (Millar) Halloran*

One day, as the brother and sister approached the breakwater on their way home, Ozzie Mackinley called out to Barbara. "Come on over here, dear, and see what we've got fer ya!"

Barbara ambled toward the small hut Mackinley shared with his wife during the lobster season. Grace Mackinley was sunning on a chair just outside the door of the shack. In her lap, she had a small black puppy. She smiled broadly as she offered it for Barbara to take in her arms. The pup was working with all its might to wag its white-tipped tail. Barbara reached out and took the little dog to her chest. She'd never held a puppy before. She could feel its wiggling warmth and sleek coat in her hands. As the pup ran a wet sandpaper tongue along her cheek, Barbara knew she must have it for her own.

"D'ya think yer father'll let ya bring 'er home with ya?"

George had never been quite as sober with his peers as he was with his children but, just the same, his cronies knew him to be a strict and demanding father. It happened at this moment that George was on the dock sorting out some empty lobster crates. Since he'd lost his own lobster boat to a storm back in 1940, George had taken up the job of weighing catches for the cannery. Barbara approached him with the puppy in her arms. The little dog had bright, friendly eyes, and white on her feet and chest. Barbara knew the white tip on her tail meant good luck. After all, she'd read lots of stories about dogs.

It took George a few moments to acknowledge his daughter standing beside him. It would have been difficult for him to miss her presence, though, since the dock was quiet at this time of day. Finally, he swiveled his head from the stoop he'd taken on in order to examine the wooden boxes.

"What'cha got there, then?"

Barbara held out the fat puppy, still wriggling in her hands. "Can I take her home?"

George took a moment to straighten up to his full height. He couldn't do that as fast as he used to, and he rubbed the back of his neck as he regarded his blonde-haired daughter. Then he folded his arms to appraise from a distance the shiny black coat of the puppy. It looked healthy enough.

"Don't you think we have enough animals to take care of already?"

The question wasn't a refusal, and Barbara took advantage of the opening. "I can look after her, Daddy. You'll see."

George put a hand up to his chin, as though he were giving the proposal some hard thought. "What's your mother going to say?"

"She'll say I can have her if you do. I promise I'll look after her. I'll call her Lassie!"

George was still rubbing his chin. "How do you know you can look after a dog? It'd have to be trained, too."

Her father's brows were knitting together the way they often did when he was about to make a judgment. Barbara knew this would be her last chance to persuade him.

"I can do it, Daddy. I'll train her to do all kinds of things. She'll be good! Look at her! Isn't she pretty?"

Barbara was holding the puppy out for her father to take a closer look, but George turned back to his work.

"Tell your mother I said you can keep it, but you'll have to give it half your food."

Barbara was ecstatic. She hugged the puppy to her as she ran toward the breakwater where David was getting the boat ready to row home. From that day forward Lassie was a member of the Millar family. She swam, sailed, climbed ladders, rode horseback, and had her own chair to sit on whenever she was in the house.

Lassie lived to the ripe old age of seventeen and a half. By the way, she did get her own food, not mine.
—Barbara Millar

Meanwhile, Ruth was readjusting to life in a lighthouse. It seemed ironic now, having been on the mainland for so long, that a house named for the light it gave did not itself have electricity. There were rumours that electrification was on its way to Bayfield, but it would never reach this house. There was also the matter of the distance to the well, especially with Ruth's hands not as strong as they used to be. But she could cope. Long before they'd gone to the mainland, she had dispensed with her old washboard and Eureka tub. She now had a washing machine with a lever-operated agitator and a wringer that worked with a hand crank—this was a luxury. She also had all of her familiar things around her again, like her mother's handed-down china, her pump organ, and the sounds of the sea through the open windows. There were worse ways to live.

George, though, was looking forward to retirement. Somehow, the trip by rowboat between breakwater and island took longer than he remembered. His arms and shoulders had to be re-accustomed to pulling the oars through water, and the walk between the landing and the house did not go as well as it used to now that he had a game heel. Then there were the backaches, and while he'd always had those, they kept him laid up longer than they used to. Still, he'd have nothing stronger for them than the Dodd's Kidney Pills and Minard's Liniment he'd always kept on hand. Anything else was foolishness. A man should be able to handle his own pain.

Ruth had known when they returned to the island that their days in the place were numbered. Ever since 1939, George had been keeping a weather eye out for a good house on the mainland. In 1949, he finally found one. It was the former home of the Hulberts, across the road from St. Matthew's United Church in Afton. David was given almost sole charge of the property until he joined the Royal Canadian Navy in 1952. For the next two years, Ruth, Barbara, and Lassie adopted a routine of living in the Afton house for the school term and moving back to the island in the summer. George would stay with the light until it closed down in November, and then he and the cat—his only companion on the island—would join life on the mainland until navigation resumed in April. Each fall and again each spring, the livestock would be moved between the mainland farm and the island.

By late 1959, the Millar household was almost completely shifted to Afton, and with Barbara having left to attend nursing school in 1954, its occupants were down to George, Ruth, Lassie, and the cats. It was time for George to retire. He wouldn't miss the job, really. Life on the island had become generally more difficult from year to year, and the obligation to keep the light burning at all costs had a way of tying one down. George was looking forward to knowing what it felt like to be free from duty, a feeling he'd never experienced. Already, he and Ruth were planning the first of what they hoped would be many cross-Canada tours in a new Volkswagen bus.

Still, there was something nagging at George and Ruth about leaving the island behind. It wasn't that there was going to be an automatic light from now on, or that it would be housed in a brand new tower. These facts they accepted—welcomed even—as marks of progress in a fast-changing world. It was not knowing what was going to happen to the old lighthouse that worried them. They couldn't just leave it there. They couldn't let a home that had echoed with so much life for so long just sag and die on its own, like some forgotten old nag in a field.

> They had become quite attached to Lassie, but she was a bit blind and quite deaf and starting to lose the use of her hind legs. One day Dad decided that he would get some chloroform and end her misery, but somehow he managed to drop the bottle and break it. He blamed it on the bottle's thin glass.
> —David Millar

After George retired in April 1960, the old lighthouse was declared "surplus" by the federal government and put up for sale. George tried to help his former superiors find someone who might want to buy it and move it to the mainland, but the move would likely prove more trouble than it was worth. The only other remedy for surplus government property was destruction. As the winter of 1961 closed in without any buyers, George considered that he might have to do it himself. "Much as I hate to see the old house wrecked, I am willing to co-operate with you to this end, if it is your wish for me to do so," he wrote to the district engineer in Charlottetown.

But it would be a big job, and there would not be much to salvage from the lighthouse that would be useful on the farm in Afton. George was sixty-four, and he would likely have to hire someone to help. The response came little more than a week later from P. J. Gleeson in Charlottetown: "We have reviewed this matter again and now consider that it might be better for us to undertake this work with our own forces at some time next summer since…it might mean that you would suffer a considerable loss if you undertook to do the work."

There were still some belongings in the house that George had intended to bring to the mainland when he got a chance. They were mostly keepsakes, though, with no practical purpose, so he did not rush to remove them. The next summer, George and Ruth set off for their first cross-Canada tour in their Volkswagen bus, christened Samantha after the Millar tradition of naming important additions to the household. They gave little thought to their former home as the new wheels touched pavement on the Trans-Canada Highway. They were beginning to enjoy freedom from obligation, and from the maxim, "wind and weather permitting," that had ruled their lives for most of the previous thirty-five years.

It wasn't until George and Ruth returned in October that they learned the lighthouse had been torn down and burned, along with everything they'd left inside. Suddenly, the practicality of these articles became clear. They were reminders of earlier times: the Aladdin lamp that had illuminated school work at the dining room table; books the children had saved for and collected over the years; the miniature table and chairs given by the grandparents; the play tea set that had followed; and the only known photograph of George as a child. They were touchstones to earlier times, artifacts from stages of life that could never be lived again. They were signposts that said "the Millars were here." Now they were gone, and no amount of recrimination or regret could bring them back.

Whether they liked it or not, the transition from Pomquet Island was complete: George and Ruth were mainlanders like everyone else. As mementoes, George had kept a few old lightkeeper's diaries in which daily weather conditions, the "time of lighting" and "time of extinguishing" had been precisely recorded. Ruth kept some of the photos she had taken over the years. But "their" island wasn't theirs any more. Nothing was left to draw them back, and even if there were, George had given up the boat that could take them there.

Sixteen years after the Pomquet Island lighthouse was put to rest, Barbara and Thelma were standing with their father in the living room of the Afton home. They could see, through the windows of Ruth's plant-crowded sun porch, neighbours and former schoolmates gathering in the churchyard across the road. It was Sunday and, as usual, George was dressed in his grey trousers and navy blazer with the Royal Canadian Legion crest on the breast pocket. What was most unusual about this day was not the presence of his two daughters at the same time, it was the absence of his wife. She was in the hospital in Antigonish, only just beginning to recover from a stroke.

George's shoulders were bent permanently. The years of back pain had given him a distinct stoop. His dark hair and moustache were still as bushy as always, but grey was displacing black more and more each year. He wore glasses and his walk was closer to a shuffle than it had ever been. George was in his eighties and, for the first time in nearly sixty years, he did not have Ruth by his side.

In one hand George held the envelope for the collection plate, like the ones he and Ruth had placed there every Sunday for fifty-odd years. He was standing in the living room, waiting for the mantel clock to strike the quarter-hour, the signal that it was time to start the short walk to church in order to be there just in time for some chit-chat before the service. Today, everyone would want to know about Ruth.

The three stood quietly, biding their time, with only the ticking of the clock to break the silence. Thelma was turned toward the sun porch, staring absently at one of her mother's geraniums and thinking that it could use some pinching back. The whole array of plants could probably use a good watering and clipping. She would do that after church. This was not something George would do himself, but it was something he might expect to happen. Besides, the chore would keep Thelma from having to think up conversation with her father.

A soft whirring, followed by a single *gong* signalled 10:45—time to depart. When the clock sounded, it was 10:45, and time to depart. Thelma turned back from the window and looked to George for a signal to start for the door. Instead, she saw him standing—suspended almost—with both hands dangling by his sides. He didn't seem to know what to do. When he raised his gaze toward her, Thelma saw that, behind his glasses, his eyes were wet, and that each cheek bore a silvery trail. She glanced toward Barbara. Her sister had seen it, too. Their father was allowing them a glimpse into his heart, but there was nothing either of them could say.

George held out the envelope toward his eldest daughter. "Here," he said gruffly. "You take this. I can't face them today."

Thelma took the envelope and George turned away. The sisters watched as he shuffled out of the room, wrestling off his jacket as he went. All his life, George had been casting off the weight and running the race of life with patience, just as it said in his daily prayer. He couldn't cast off the weight today, though. He needed Ruth to help him do it, and she wasn't there.

Ruth would be remembering her own prayer more often from now on:

"God, grant me the serenity
To accept the things I cannot change…"

It would take her some time to regain full speech, and she knew she could no longer count on her health. Her bones were becoming more and more brittle by the year, and she couldn't risk a fall. Already, she knew—although she would never ask a doctor to confirm it—that her spine was beginning to crumble. Her eyesight was going, too. The glaucoma was closing in more each year. The arthritis in her hands was making it hard to do even the simplest of chores, and both she and George were falling deafer all the time. Even the hearing aids weren't much help to Ruth anymore.

Ruth and George were going to have to start accepting help, and the change would not go smoothly. A few years later they spent the winter with Rosa and her husband, Ralph, in Pugwash. It was an unhappy time. Retired for a few years herself, Rosa had already taken on her in-laws, Harry and Laura Mattinson—it had been their house after all. Harry was bedridden, recuperating from a broken hip, and Laura's health was failing, too. The place was physically big enough for two sets of in-laws, along with Rosa and Ralph, but, as it turned out, no house was big enough for the senior Millars and the senior Mattinsons together.

Having resigned herself to a life of caring for her elderly family—first her grandparents and now her own parents and her husband's parents—Rosa knew it would not be an easy winter. What she did not count on was the outright competition for her attention. When she was growing up, she got along with her brothers and sisters out of necessity. There was no jockeying for positions of favour with her parents or with anyone else. But here in Rosa's house, it was almost a battleground. If she brought a cup of tea for Laura, she would have to bring one for Ruth, too. If she sat down to watch TV with Harry, that would be the time George would need her to help him with something. Sometimes, when they were all together, Rosa felt as though she could cut the air with a knife.

After a few months, George and Ruth determined they were fit enough to return to Afton and live on their own—at least for the summer. Rosa felt some measure of relief when this announcement was made, although she worried about her parents, having been close at hand to observe their individual frailties.

On the day that George and Ruth prepared to embark on the long drive back to Afton, Rosa almost meant it when she said to her father, "If you find that it gets to be too much, you can always come back here."

George was wrestling a suitcase into the back of his bright red and yet-unnamed truck, which had replaced Samantha. The Volkswagen bus was now retired to the back of the woodshed in Afton. Rosa had raised her voice so that George could hear even though he had his back to her. She was accustomed to this, since everyone in the house except Ralph had some degree of deafness.

When he didn't answer, she said it again, a little louder: "If it's too much for you back in Afton, you can always come back here."

"Hum-m-pf!" said George. He'd heard her all right. "This is the last place I'd come back to!"

George may have intended the insult for Harry and Laura. But it brought back to Rosa those stinging childhood snubs: she was supposed to be a boy, she'd not been good enough to start grade two with Thelma. To George, she'd always been "the cold susceptible." Rosa had her arms folded against the chill April morning and, at his reply, hugged herself a little closer. Without a word, she turned and went back into the house. Rosa saw her mother out the kitchen door and helped her carry her things to the truck, but she was not there with Ralph in the driveway to wave her parents goodbye.

There was no miracle, as George may have hoped, that would have made it possible for he and Ruth to stay on the farm in Afton the next winter. Instead, they spent the next two winters in a boarding house in Lower South River, not far from Afton. But when Ruth broke her hip the second year, they both knew it was time to look for something more permanent. As soon as there was an opening at the East Cumberland Lodge nursing home in Pugwash, they moved in. But George was beginning to tire of the race. He contracted pneumonia in the summer of 1982 and, one August night, died in his sleep.

The day was washed in late-summer rain as he was lowered into the ground in the cemetery behind St. Matthew's United Church in Afton. The funeral had been a lengthy process, with a service at the funeral home in Pugwash, a separate Royal Canadian Legion service, and a procession all the way to the cemetery. Having been ready for some time, the hole where he would be buried had begun to accumulate water, and the freshly turned-up earth beside it was slick. Car tires and smooth-soled shoes slid on wet grass. Mourners tried to fit under too few umbrellas by the gravesite as the last words were said over George Millar.

Ruth did not stand by the graveside. She sat quietly out of the rain, unable to walk without help. She bore it all—the funeral services, the reception—with an impassive face. She barely spoke. Hardly able to hear, she found it too much effort to make conversation with the people who had come to share her grief. It would not do to cry on this day. She would save that for later, when no one was looking. Then she would cry for George, and for the life they were leaving behind.

Very gradually from that day forward, life ceased to hold purpose for Ruth. On a stormy January day in 1985, she slipped quietly away. She was laid to rest beside George in Afton the following summer.

The race was over.

There is no longer a lightkeeper on Pomquet Island. The flashing white light in the new tower is operated by batteries…the dwelling and out-buildings were razed to the ground and burned. Our Pomquet Island as we knew it is no more. —George Millar

EPILOGUE

*A*ll that remains today of the original Pomquet Island lighthouse are the cellar and the concrete cistern that was installed in 1937. The cliff on which the lighthouse sat has eroded considerably over the years, so that it is no longer as steep as it was when the Millars lived there. The foundation itself is now perilously close to the edge of the bank.

There is no longer any trace of the barn, the woodshed, the outhouse, the pigpen, the chicken coop, or the oil house. All were torn down, burned, and cleared away along with the lighthouse on

October 4, 1962. The well, which was located a good distance away from the buildings, remained open for forty-four years, but was covered in 2006. The track from the landing to the lighthouse site has long since grown over with trees and shrubs, but the trees that once covered about two-thirds of the island have begun to die, due to the acidic droppings of cormorants.

Pomquet Island has been almost completely reclaimed by cormorants, great blue herons, and seagulls, which nest there by the hundreds. For a time the island—with the exception of a small piece of land on which the current automated light sits—was owned by an American family, who purchased it from the federal government. A small weathered shed remains near the centre of the island as a reminder of their tenure. A family member later turned the island over to the Nature Conservancy of Canada.

This unwatched light tower now serves the fishermen of Bayfield Harbour. Built in the familiar white, salt-shaker style with a red roof, it stands fifty feet from the old lighthouse site. Erected in 1959, it can be found on navigation charts at latitude 45° 39' 27", longtitude 61° 44' 54". The tower is twenty feet high and thirty feet above sea level with a battery-powered white light that flashes every four seconds over a range of six nautical miles.

It has been more than eighty years since the Millar family took up lightkeeping, and more than forty-five years have passed since the island was inhabited year-round. Despite the passage of time, Pomquet Island remains an abiding and fundamental influence on all six of George and Ruth Millar's children.

After Thelma began her nursing career, she moved to Prince Edward Island. There, through a long-time pen pal from the Maple Leaf Club, she met Roland Beairsto, a farmer who lived in West Covehead. They married in 1953 and had three children: John Keir, Susan, and Ruth. Roland died in December 1989, and Thelma now lives in Bowmanville, Ontario, near her daughters.

While Rosa was living in Pugwash with her grandparents, she met Ralph Mattinson, who joined the RCAF. They married in 1944 and, with their three children, Keith, Janet, and Jennifer, lived on a number of military bases in the Maritimes and Ontario before their retirement to Pugwash. Ralph died in April 1985. Rosa still lives in the old Mattinson family home there.

Managing a mainland woodlot, cutting firewood, and ferrying it annually to Pomquet Island developed in Malcolm an interest in forestry. After his discharge from the RCAF, he studied forestry at the University of New Brunswick. From there, he went to work for the Department of Natural Resources in Saskatchewan. In 1951, he married Geraldine (Gerry) Perry, and they settled near Peter Pond near Prince Albert. Gerry died in 2003. Malcolm and his fiancée Jeanette Schuler now divide their time between Peter Pond and Saskatoon.

After graduating from grade twelve and before beginning her teaching career, Minna worked for the owner of a grocery store and hotel in the small community of Monastery. There she met Damien (Andy) Halloran. They were married and had three children: Karen, Karla, and Scott. Also a member of the RCAF, Andy had numerous postings, including two to Germany, before retiring to George and Ruth's former home in Afton. Andy died in 2005. Minna still lives in the house across the road from St. Matthew's United Church.

The sea was in David's blood, so in 1952 he joined the Royal Canadian Navy. Some years later, a shipmate introduced him to Eileen Ryan. After they were married, she gave birth to identical triplets, David, Donald, and Dale. They were followed, one at a time, by Donna, Susan, Christine, and much later by Shawn. David and Eileen live in Dartmouth.

Barbara was the last child to grow up on Pomquet Island. In the summer of 1953, she took a job in Antigonish, only to return to Afton

> *There are other things I remember. The way the ice piled up in winter. Coasting down the field and onto the ice. How I learned to like reading, writing letters, walking in the woods and learning about the flowers.*
> *—Barbara Millar*

in the fall. Early the following year, she entered nursing school in Halifax, thus ending her contact with lightkeeping life. Never married, Barbara has worked and lived in the Halifax–Dartmouth area ever since.

SELECTED BIBLIOGRAPHY

Baird, David M. *Northern Lights: Lighthouses of Canada.* Toronto: Lynx
   Images Inc, 1999.
Bird, Will R. "Nova Scotia Has Many Lights." *Canadian Geographical
   Journal,* 54 (March 1957): 90-103.
Budge, Billy. *Memoirs of a Lightkeeper's Son.* Lawrencetown, N.S.:
   Pottersfield, 2003.
Bush, Edward F. "Beacon lights on Canadian Shores." *Canadian
   Geographical Journal,* 22-29. Vol. 90, No. 2: 1975.

Bush, Edward F. *The Canadian Lighthouse.* Manuscript Report No. 58. Ottawa: Department of Indian Affairs and Northern Development, 1970.

Dixon, Conrad. *Basic Coastal Navigation.* London: Adlard Coles Limited, 1968.

Gaunt, Arthur. "Beacons of the Seven Seas." *Canadian Geographical Journal,* 36:16-21, 1948.

"The lightkeeper goes out." *The Globe and Mail,* January 3, 2004, F8.

Guichard, Jean, and Ken Trethewey. *North Atlantic Lighthouses.* Paris: Flammarion, 2002.

Irwin, Rip. *Lighthouses and Lights of Nova Scotia.* Halifax: Nimbus, 2003.

James, Terry. *In Praise of Oxen.* Halifax: Nimbus, 1992.

Millar, George E. "Thirty-five Years a Light Keeper." *Chief and Petty Officers' Bulletin.* Stadacona, NS: 1962.

Millar, Ruth E. "Ruth Reminisces: An Interesting Account of the Vimy Pilgrimage." *Oxford Journal.* Oxford: 1937.

Mills, Chris. *Vanishing Lights.* Hantsport, Nova Scotia: Lancelot, 1992.

———. *Lighthouse Legacies: Stories of Nova Scotia's Lightkeeping Families.* Halifax: Nimbus, 2006.

Ozorak, Paul. *Abandoned Military Installations of Canada.* Vol. 3, Atlantic, 2001.

Richardson, Evelyn M. *We Keep a Light.* Halifax: Nimbus, 1995.

Stanley-Blackwell, Laurie C. C., and R. A. MacLean. *Historic Antigonish: Town and Country.* Halifax: Nimbus, 2004.

Stephens, David E. *Lighthouses of Nova Scotia.* Windsor, Nova Scotia: Lancelot, 1973.

Thompson, Courtney. *Lighthouses of Atlantic Canada.* Mt. Desert, Maine: CatNap, 2000.

Weems, P. V. H., and Lee, C. V. *Marine Navigation.* 2nd ed. Annapolis, Maryland: Weems System of Navigation, 1958.

Witney, Dudley. *The Lighthouse.* Toronto: McClelland and Stewart, 1975.

INDEX